Enterprise Advanced Routing and Services
ENARSI 300-410 V1.0 Concentration Exam

1st Edition

Copyright © 2021 CCIEin8Weeks

ISBN: 9798704540182

Contents at a Glance

Chapter 1 Layer 3 Technologies
Chapter 2 VPN Technologies
Chapter 3 Infrastructure Security
Chapter 4 Infrastructure Services

Table of Contents

About the Author 5

Preface 6

How to use this Study Guide 6

What's available on the CCIEin8Weeks website 7

Chapter 1 Layer 3 Technologies 8
    Troubleshoot administrative distance (all routing protocols) 10
    Troubleshoot route map for any routing protocol (attributes, tagging, filtering)..........11
    Troubleshoot loop prevention mechanisms (filtering, tagging, split horizon, route poisoning) 13
    Troubleshoot redistribution between any routing protocols or routing sources 16
    Troubleshoot manual and auto-summarization with any routing protocol 16
    Configure and verify policy-based routing 18
    Configure and verify VRF-Lite 19
    Describe Bidirectional Forwarding Detection (BFD) 25
    Troubleshoot EIGRP (classic and named mode) 27
    Troubleshoot OSPF (v2/v3) 31
    Network types, area types, and router types 32
    Path preference 35
    Troubleshoot BGP (Internal and External) 35

Chapter 2 VPN Technologies 45

Describe MPLS operations (LSR, LDP, label switching, LSP) 46
    Describe MPLS Layer 3 VPN 47

Configure and verify DMVPN (single hub) 48

Chapter 3 Infrastructure Security 58

Troubleshoot device security using IOS AAA (TACACS+, RADIUS, local database) 59

Troubleshoot router security features 60
    IPv4 access control lists (standard, extended, time-based) 60
    IPv6 Traffic Filter 62
    Unicast reverse path forwarding (uRPF) 63

Troubleshoot control plane policing (CoPP) (Telnet, SSH, HTTP(S), SNMP, EIGRP, OSPF, BGP) 64

Describe IPv6 First Hop security features (RA guard, DHCP guard, binding table, ND inspection/snooping, source guard) 70

Chapter 4 Infrastructure Services 72

Troubleshoot device management 73

Console and VTY...73

Telnet, HTTP, HTTPS, SSH, SCP, (T)FTP..73

Troubleshoot SNMP (v2c, v3) **74**

Troubleshoot network problems using logging (local, syslog, debugs, conditional debugs, timestamps)...**75**

Troubleshoot IPv4 and IPv6 DHCP (DHCP client, IOS DHCP server, DHCP relay, DHCP options)...**78**

Troubleshoot network performance issues using IP SLA (jitter, tracking objects, delay, connectivity)...**79**

Troubleshoot NetFlow (v5, v9, flexible NetFlow) **81**

Troubleshoot network problems using Cisco DNA Center assurance (connectivity, monitoring, device health, network health).............................**87**

About the Author

Muhammad Afaq Khan started his professional career at Cisco TAC San Jose and passed his first CCIE in 2002 (#9070). He held multiple technical and management positions at Cisco San Jose HQ over his 11 years of tenure at the company before moving into cloud software and data center infrastructure IT industries.

He has worked at startups as well as Fortune 100 companies in senior leadership positions over his career. He is also a published author (Cisco Press, 2009) and holds multiple patents in the areas of networking, security, and virtualization. Currently, he is a founder at Full Stack Networker and a vocal advocate for network automation technologies and NetDevOps. He is a Cisco Certified DevNet Associate1 and was among the first 500 people #DevNet500 worldwide to pass the exam.

Preface

Congratulations! You have taken your first step towards preparing and passing the Cisco Enterprise Advanced Routing and Services (ENARSI) 300-410 V1.0 Exam.

Did you just purchase a copy? **Interested in getting access to a complimentary ENARSI Exam Quiz?** Register here[1], and then send us an email at support@cciein8weeks.com to get started.

This study guide is dedicated to all *those souls who will never settle for less than they can be, do, share, and give!*

How to use this Study Guide

This guide is for anyone who's studying for Cisco ENARSI 300-410 exam. I strongly suggest taking a methodical approach for exam preparation, i.e., start with a target date or when you would like to sit for the actual exam and then work backwards to see what kind of study plan would work for you. To augment this study guide, I have put together a 65-hour learning plan[2] consisting entirely of public resources, something that you can download today and follow along.

ENARSI 300-410 V1.0 Exam Topics Bodies of Knowledge	Exam Weight
Layer 3 Technologies	35%
VPN Technologies	20%
Infrastructure Security	20%
Infrastructure Services	25%

---

[1] cciein8weeks.com/user-account

[2] https://bit.ly/2O8IWuF

What's available on the CCIEin8Weeks website

CCIEin8Weeks.com carries the supplemental resources (sold separately) that go hand in hand with this study guide to further ensure your exam success.

- Exam Prep Bundle[3] that covers all bodies of knowledge tested on the ENARSI Exam
- 4x Practice Quizzes (one for each section as per the official curriculum)
- 1x Practice Exam (to help you prepare to face the pressure of a real Cisco exam)

---

[3] https://bit.ly/3cEkDP7

Chapter 1 Layer 3 Technologies

This chapter covers the following exam topics from Cisco's official Enterprise Advanced Routing and Services (ENARSI) 300-410 V1.0 exam blueprint.

- Troubleshoot administrative distance (all routing protocols)
- Troubleshoot route map for any routing protocol (attributes, tagging, filtering)
- Troubleshoot loop prevention mechanisms (filtering, tagging, split horizon, route poisoning)
- Troubleshoot redistribution between any routing protocols or routing sources
- Troubleshoot manual and auto-summarization with any routing protocol
- Configure and verify policy-based routing
- Configure and verify VRF-Lite
- Describe Bidirectional Forwarding Detection
- Troubleshoot EIGRP (classic and named mode)
    - Address families (IPv4, IPv6)
    - Neighbor relationship and authentication
    - Loop-free path selections (RD, FD, FC, successor, feasible successor, stuck in active)
    - Stubs
    - Load balancing (equal and unequal cost)
    - Metrics
- Troubleshoot OSPF (v2/v3)
    - Address families (IPv4, IPv6)
    - Neighbor relationship and authentication
    - Network types, area types, and router types
        - Point-to-point, multipoint, broadcast, non-broadcast
        - Area type: backbone, normal, transit, stub, NSSA, totally stub
        - Internal router, backbone router, ABR, ASBR
        - Virtual link
    - Path preference

- Troubleshoot BGP (Internal and External)
  - Address families (IPv4, IPv6)
  - Neighbor relationship and authentication (next-hop, multi-hop, 4-byte AS, private AS, route refresh, synchronization, operation, peer group, states and timers)
  - Path preference (attributes and best-path)
  - Route reflector (excluding multiple route reflectors, confederations, dynamic peer)
  - Policies (inbound/outbound filtering, path manipulation)

Troubleshoot administrative distance (all routing protocols)

Administrative distance (or AD) is a number that an IP routing device uses as a tie breaker when selecting a best path, to a given destination, when two or more paths exists from two or more different routing protocols or sources. During this comparison, the lowest AD value always prevails.

AD values can range from 0 (most preferred) to 255 (least preferred). Every vendor has its own default AD values assigned to each routing protocol however they can be customized by the network engineer as desired. AD is an indication of reliability or a measure of route preference of the given routing source.

Below is a comparison of Cisco and Juniper default AD values.

Routing Source	Cisco AD	Juniper AD
Directly connected interfaces	0	0
Static route with exit interface	1	5
Static route with next-hop IP address	1	5
EIGRP summary route	5	n/a
BGP (Internal/External)	20/200	170/170
EIGRP (Internal/External)	90	n/a
OSPF (Internal/External)	110/150	10
IS-IS (L1/L2 Internal)	115/115	15/18
IS-IS (L1/L2 External)	115/115	160/165
RIP	120	100
Unknown	255	

Both Cisco and Juniper allow one-line configuration to customize a default AD value for a given routing protocol. In order to override the default AD value, you can simply go to routing process or configuration mode, and then issue "distance <new-AD>" or "set protocols <protocol> group <group-number> preference <new-AD>" on Cisco IOS and Juniper Junos OS devices respectively. Please note that there are other ways to change AD values.

For troubleshooting, it is imperative to know the main reasons behind why AD values are modified by the network engineers in the first place. There are three most common reasons that are worth noting here.

- Route redistribution
- Network migration from one routing protocol to another
- Using static route as a backup to an existing IGP route

Troubleshoot route map for any routing protocol (attributes, tagging, filtering)

Route maps come in handy during IP routing redistribution as a way to select (or filter) some routes from a given routing source and redistribute them into another routing source.

There are three main components of route-map configuration in this context, i.e.

- Matching criteria defined by match statement(s), e.g. matching on an IP ACL
- Setting criteria defined by set statements(s), e.g. setting metric value, type etc.
- Application or attachment via "redistribute <routing-protocol> <#> subnets route-map <route-map-name>" command.

Let's now try this out with an example network topology. Assuming we have properly configured OSPF and EIGRP on each routing domain and now we're tasked to mutually redistributing those routes using route-maps.

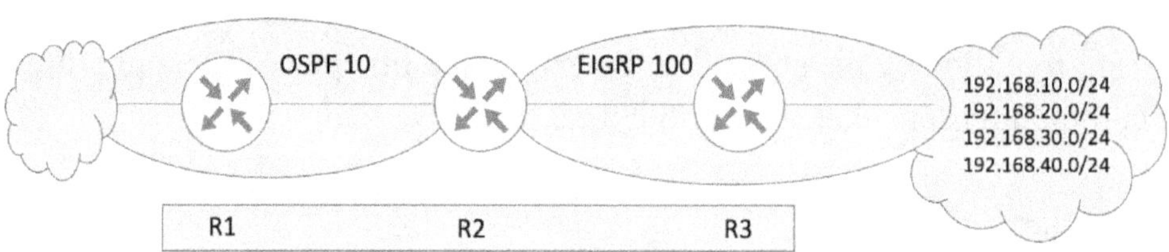

The objective is to only redistribute networks 192.168.10.0/24 and 192.168.20.0/24 into OSPF and advertise them as external type 1 (E1) routes with an external metric of 20. In order to achieve our goal, we need to configure and apply route-map on R2, the redistribution point.

```
R2(config)#access-list 10 permit 192.168.10.0 0.0.0.255
R2(config)#access-list 10 permit 192.168.20.0 0.0.0.255
R2(config)#route-map CCIEin8Weeks permit 10
R2(config-route-map)#match ip address 10
R2(config-route-map)#set metric 20
R2(config-route-map)#set metric-type type-1
R2(config)#router ospf 10
R2(config)#redistribute eigrp 100 subnets route-map CCIEin8Weeks
```

Please note that 192.168.30.0/24 and 192.168.40.0/24 will not be redistributed because of the implicit deny any at the end of the route map ACL.

In a two-way multipoint redistribution, you can use route-map tagging for route selection and filtering.

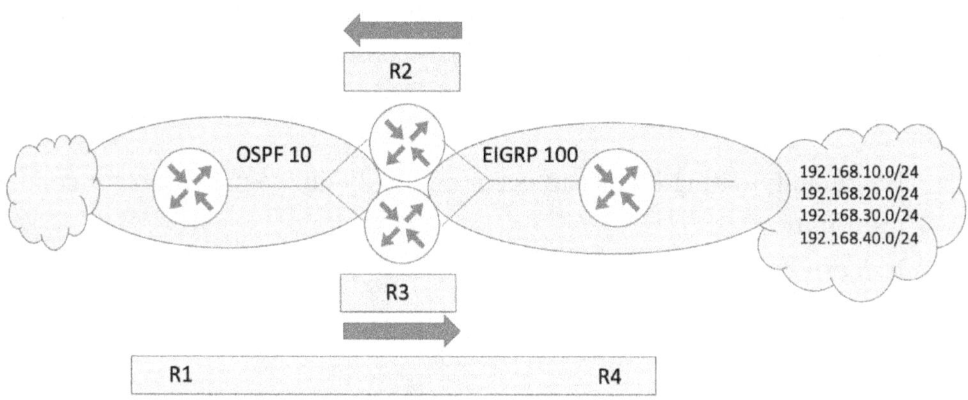

R2(config)#route-map EIGRP-to-OSPF deny 10
R2(config-route-map)#match tag 66

R2(config-route-map)#route-map EIGRP-to-OSPF permit 20
R2(config-route-map)#set tag 33

R2(config-route-map)#router ospf 10
R2(config-router)#redistribute eigrp 100 subnets route-map EIGRP-to-OSPF

Please note that you will need to apply a similar route-map configuration to R3 in order to filter OSPF to EIGRP routes.

Route maps are powerful tools when it comes to redistribution of routes. They allow network engineers to apply very fine but specific changes to routing information when it is redistributed between routing protocols. While troubleshooting route-map misconfigurations in routing applications, you're likely to find issues related to suboptimal routing or even traffic blackholing.

Troubleshoot loop prevention mechanisms (filtering, tagging, split horizon, route poisoning)

We've already discussed filtering with distribute-list as well tagging with route maps. Distance Vector Protocols (or DVRs) are based on Bellman-Ford algorithm which has several limitations.

- By default, routing loops can occur endlessly due to provision for count-to-infinity
- It doesn't scale well, so can't be used in a very large network
- Topology change is propagated slowly, i.e. router to router as opposed to flooding

In order to mitigate above issues that are inherent in DVRs, a number of features were added later on to DVRs such as RIP.

Split Horizon

Split horizon is a mechanism to prevent routing loops in distance vector routing protocols such as RIP or IGRP. The underlying principle of operation works by never sending or advertising a route back onto the interface from which it was received or learned.

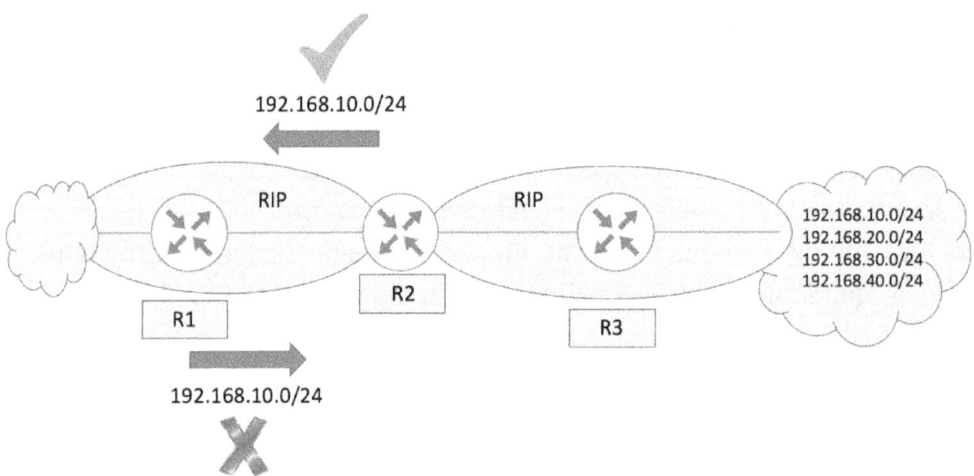

As shown in the topology above, R1 receives 192.168.10.0 from R2, but will not send the route back to R2.

Route poisoning is a method in which a router running DVR will advertise an infinity metric (16 hops in RIP) for failed routes.

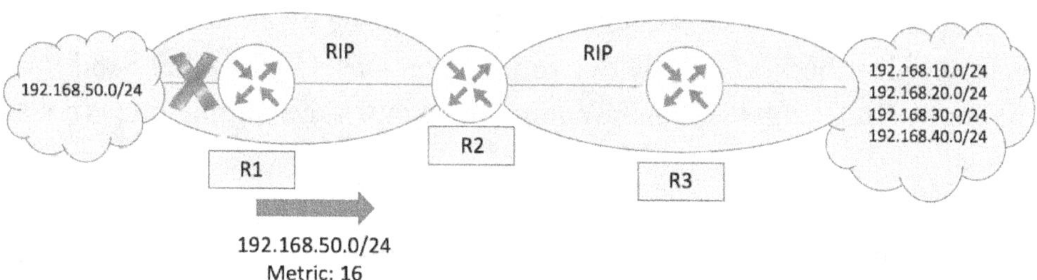

Split horizon is more effective when used with route poisoning. RIP uses both split horizon with route poisoning and hold-down timers to avoid loop formation.

Let's now summarize the loop avoidance and prevention mechanisms used by various routing protocols. You can troubleshoot routing loops using the information presented in the following table.

Routing Protocol	Loop Avoidance Feature	Loop Prevention Feature
RIP v1/v2	Split Horizon Poison Reverse Triggered Updates (v2 only)	Count to Infinity Hold-down Timers
EIGRP	Split Horizon Poison Reverse	Feasibility Condition (DUAL algorithm)
OSPF intra-area	None. SPF algorithm inherently prevents loops.	
OSPF inter-area	Split Horizon (like distance vector protocols)	
IS-IS	SPF algorithm and reliable flooding	

eBGP (Inter-AS)	AS Path (attribute)	
iBGP (Intra-AS)	Split Horizon	Full-mesh requirement

Troubleshoot redistribution between any routing protocols or routing sources

In case of redistribution, your goal is to avoid both sub-optimal routing as well as AD related issues. You can avoid sub-optimal routing by eliminating multiple points of redistribution between two routing domains. On the other hand, avoiding AD related issues can be summarized into a few simple rules (not an exhaustive list).

- **Do not announce the routing information originally received from a routing source back into the same source** (e.g. RIP to IGRP, and then IGRP to RIP). You can easily filter routes using distribute-list. You can also avoid this by assigning tags to routes from a given routing source (such as RIP routes coming into EIGRP) and then filter using route-maps during redistribution (such as EIGRP routes coming back into RIP).
- **Always set a default-metric value during redistribution** (e.g. EIGRP metric) to avoid sub-optimal routing. EIGRP uses five different variables (or coefficients) for metric calculation but they are not set by default during redistribution (e.g. RIP to EIGRP) or for redistribute routes. This technique can also be used when redistribution is done between two processes of a same routing protocol (e.g. EIGRP) running on same or two different routers.
- **Avoid redistributing eBGP routes directly into an IGP**. In order to avoid this, you can simply use iBGP or another routing protocol.

Troubleshoot manual and auto-summarization with any routing protocol

Route summarization is a way to represent multiple networks with a single prefix in the form of a summary address. It comes handy in a large network where summarization can reduce both route update traffic as well as local resource consumption on the device.

There are two types of summarization techniques.
- Automatic summarization
- Manual summarization

Automatic summarization is where a router running a routing protocol that supports auto summarization feature (such as EIGRP or RIP) summarizes a set of routes on classful boundary. Auto summary feature is disabled by default with EIGRP (enabled by default with RIPv2), however it can be enabled/disabled by configuring "auto-summary" or "no auto-summary" commands respectively. Link state routing protocols such as OSPF and IS-IS do not support auto summarization.

Manual summarization is where a network engineer configures a route summary based on his/her own knowledge. The feature is available across the board with RIPv2, EIGRP, OSPF and IS-IS protocols.

Routing Protocol	Auto Summarization Support (Classful only)	Auto Summarization Default State (Classful only)	Manual/Classless Summarization Support
RIPv2	Yes	Enabled	Yes
EIGRP	Yes	Disabled	Yes
OSPF	No	n/a	Yes
IS-IS	No	n/a	Yes

When troubleshooting summarization related issues, keep the following key points in mind.

- If subnets of summary routes don't exist in the routing table, then the router will not generate a summary route (e.g. EIGRP)
- If the summary route is too broad and includes non-existent subnets, that can lead to a routing loop.

Configure and verify policy-based routing

Policy-based Routing (or PBR) is a feature which allows network engineers or admins to override the default routing policy with the help of a route map. PBR takes precedence over default destination-based routing mechanisms such as routing protocols.

To enable PBR, you need to create and apply a route-map. The route-map construct includes the matching criteria and the resulting action should successful matching occur. Route-maps are applied to router interface(s).

```
ip access-list standard A-LIST
permit 192.168.10.0 0.0.0.255


route-map CCIEin8Weeks permit 10
match ip address ACL
set ip next-hop 10.0.0.1


interface fa0/0
ip policy route-map CCIEin8Weeks
```

You can verify your route-map configuration using "show route-map" command.

```
# sh route-map
route-map CCIEin8Weeks, permit, sequence 10
 Match clauses:
 ip address (access-lists): A-LIST
 Set clauses:
 ip next-hop 10.0.0.1
 Policy routing matches: 0 packets, 0 bytes
```

You can verify whether your route-map actually policy routing or not by sending some pings that would match your access-list and then repeating "show route-map" command.

sh route-map
route-map CCIEin8Weeks, permit, sequence 10
 Match clauses:
 ip address (access-lists): A-LIST
 Sct clauses:
 ip next-hop 10.0.0.1
 Policy routing matches: 6 packets, 192 bytes

Configure and verify VRF-Lite

Virtual Routing and Forwarding (or VRF) is feature universally available on all modern routers and L3 switches that allows multiple instances of a routing table. The VRF achieves the virtualization of the networking devices at network layer or L3. However, in order to create a VPN, you need to interconnect individual devices that are using VRFs.

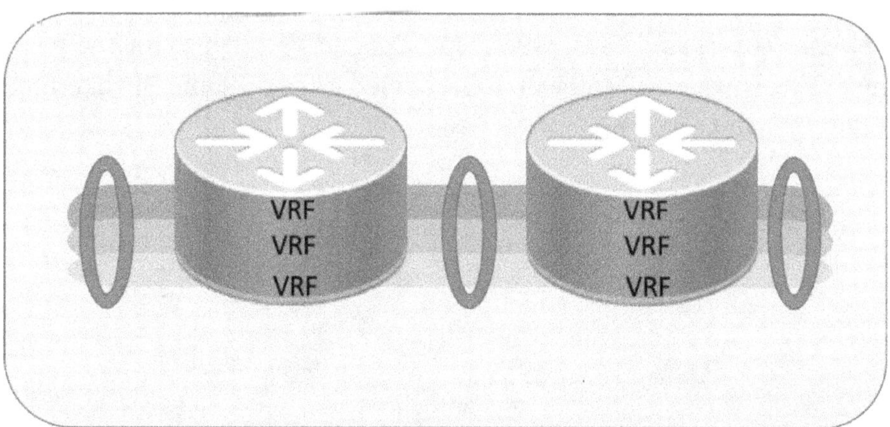

The type of data path virtualization technology to use varies depending on how far VRFs and corresponding devices are from each other. If virtualized devices are directly connected or L2 adjacent or single hop away, you have no choice but to use link or interface level virtualization e.g. using 802.1Q tag or L2 based labeling in the form of VRF to VLAN mapping.

If the virtualized devices are multiple hops away from each other, you need to use some form of tunneling to realize end to end data path virtualization. MPLS VPNs and GRE tunnels are two options that can be used to realize an end to end data path isolation. When VRFs are configured without MPLS, they are known as VRF-lite. This form of VRF configuration requires that VRF-lite interfaces are L3 or routed.

With or without MPLS, you need to understand the three device roles that the entire VRF configuration revolves around, i.e. Customer Edge (or CE), Provider Edge (or PE) and Provider (or P) devices. CE routers advertise and learn routes via CE-PE link. PE routers exchange routing information with CE routers via static routes or using a dynamic routing protocol such as BGP or RIP. PE routers only maintain VPN routes to which they are directly connected to and not all the provider's VPNs. Each VPN on PE is mapped a corresponding VRF. Finally, P routers which are also known as core routers, only reside within the provider's cloud and thus never directly attach to any of the CE routers.

With VRF-lite, multiple customers can share one CE router and one CE-PE physical link. This shared CE router keeps separate VRF tables for each customer. This is where a Multi-VRF CE device takes on some PE-like functions i.e., ability to maintain separate VRF tables.

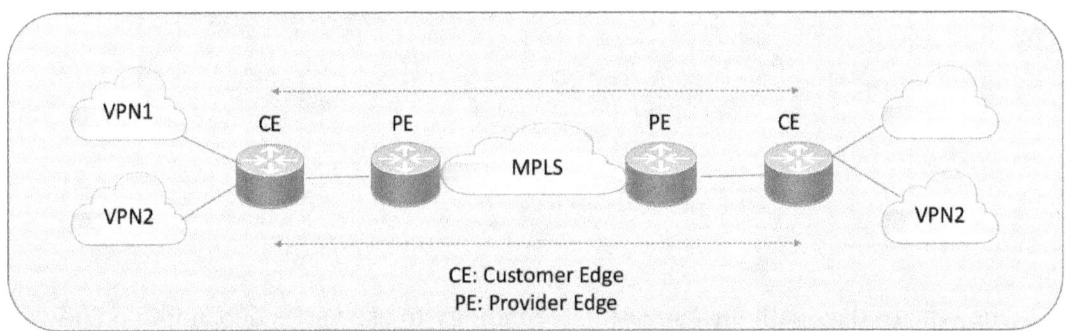

Let's go over the day in the life of a packet for a typical VRF/VPN configuration shown above.

- CE router receives a packet, depending on the input interface the packet was received on, the router will use the corresponding routing table to look up the destination and forward it onto the PE.
- Ingress PE receives the packet from CE, it performs a VRF lookup and if the route is found, the PE router will add an MPLS label and send it into the MPLS cloud.
- Now, when egress PE receives a packet from the network, it would strip off the MPLS label but use it to identify the correct VPN/VRF routing table.
- Finally, when the destination CE router receives a packet from the PE, it uses the input interface to look up the correct VRF routing table. The packet is forwarded into the VPN if a matching route is found.

Configuring Multi-VRF CE


```
Router# configure terminal
 Enter configuration commands, one per line.  End with CNTL/Z.
 Router(config)# ip routing
 Router(config)# ip vrf v11
 Router(config-vrf)# rd 900:1
 Router(config-vrf)# route-target export 900:1
 Router(config-vrf)# route-target import 900:1
 Router(config-vrf)# exit
 Router(config)# ip vrf v12
 Router(config-vrf)# rd 900:2
 Router(config-vrf)# route-target export 900:2
 Router(config-vrf)# route-target import 900:2
 Router(config-vrf)# exit

Router(config)# interface loopback1
```

```
Router(config-if)# ip vrf forwarding v11
Router(config-if)# ip address 9.9.1.8 255.255.255.0
Router(config-if)# exit

Router(config)# interface loopback2
Router(config-if)# ip vrf forwarding v12
Router(config-if)# ip address 9.9.2.8 255.255.255.0
Router(config-if)# exit

Router(config)# interface Vlan10
 Router(config-if)# ip vrf forwarding v11
 Router(config-if)# ip address 38.0.0.8 255.255.255.0
 Router(config-if)# exit
 Router(config)# interface Vlan20
 Router(config-if)# ip vrf forwarding v12
 Router(config-if)# ip address 93.0.0.8 255.255.255.0
 Router(config-if)# exit
 Router(config)# interface Vlan118
 Router(config-if)# ip vrf forwarding v12
 Router(config-if)# ip address 118.0.0.8 255.255.255.0
 Router(config-if)# exit
 Router(config)# interface Vlan208
 Router(config-if)# ip vrf forwarding v11
 Router(config-if)# ip address 208.0.0.8 255.255.255.0
 Router(config-if)# exit

Router(config)# router ospf 1 vrf v11
 Router(config-router)# redistribute bgp 900 subnets
 Router(config-router)# network 208.0.0.0 0.0.0.255 area 0
 Router(config-router)# exit
 Router(config)# router ospf 2 vrf v12
 Router(config-router)# redistribute bgp 900 subnets
 Router(config-router)# network 118.0.0.0 0.0.0.255 area 0
 Router(config-router)# exit
```

Router(config)# router bgp 900
 Router(config-router)# address-family ipv4 vrf vl2
 Router(config-router-af)# redistribute ospf 2 match internal
 Router(config-router-af)# neighbor 93.0.0.3 remote-as 100
 Router(config-router-af)# neighbor 93.0.0.3 activate
 Router(config-router-af)# network 9.9.2.0 mask 255.255.255.0
 Router(config-router-af)# exit
 Router(config-router)# address-family ipv4 vrf vl1
 Router(config-router-af)# redistribute ospf 1 match internal
 Router(config router-af)# ncighbor 38.0.0.3 remote-as 100
 Router(config-router-af)# neighbor 38.0.0.3 activate
 Router(config-router-af)# network 9.9.1.0 mask 255.255.255.0
 Router(config-router-af)# end

PE Configuration

Router# configure terminal
 Enter configuration commands, one per line. End with CNTL/Z.
 Router(config)# ip routing
 Router(config)# ip vrf vl1
 Router(config-vrf)# rd 900:1
 Router(config-vrf)# route-target export 900:1
 Router(config-vrf)# route-target import 900:1
 Router(config-vrf)# exit
 Router(config)# ip vrf v12
 Router(config-vrf)# rd 900:2
 Router(config-vrf)# route-target export 900:2
 Router(config-vrf)# route-target import 900:2
 Router(config-vrf)# exit

Router(config)# interface loopback1
 Router(config-if)# ip vrf forwarding vl1
 Router(config-if)# ip address 9.9.1.8 255.255.255.0

```
Router(config-if)# exit

Router(config)# interface loopback2
Router(config-if)# ip vrf forwarding v12
Router(config-if)# ip address 9.9.2.8 255.255.255.0
Router(config-if)# exit

Router(config)# interface Vlan10
Router(config-if)# ip vrf forwarding v11
Router(config-if)# ip address 38.0.0.8 255.255.255.0
Router(config-if)# exit
Router(config)# interface Vlan20
Router(config-if)# ip vrf forwarding v12
Router(config-if)# ip address 93.0.0.8 255.255.255.0
Router(config-if)# exit
Router(config)# interface Vlan118
Router(config-if)# ip vrf forwarding v12
Router(config-if)# ip address 118.0.0.8 255.255.255.0
Router(config-if)# exit
Router(config)# interface Vlan208
Router(config-if)# ip vrf forwarding v11
Router(config-if)# ip address 208.0.0.8 255.255.255.0
Router(config-if)# exit

Router(config)# router ospf 1 vrf v11
Router(config-router)# redistribute bgp 900 subnets
Router(config-router)# network 208.0.0.0 0.0.0.255 area 0
Router(config-router)# exit
Router(config)# router ospf 2 vrf v12
Router(config-router)# redistribute bgp 900 subnets
Router(config-router)# network 118.0.0.0 0.0.0.255 area 0
Router(config-router)# exit

Router(config)# router bgp 900
```

Router(config-router)# address-family ipv4 vrf vl2
Router(config-router-af)# redistribute ospf 2 match internal
Router(config-router-af)# neighbor 93.0.0.3 remote-as 100
Router(config-router-af)# neighbor 93.0.0.3 activate
Router(config-router-af)# network 9.9.2.0 mask 255.255.255.0
Router(config-router-af)# exit
Router(config-router)# address-family ipv4 vrf vl1
Router(config-router-af)# redistribute ospf 1 match internal
Router(config-router-af)# neighbor 38.0.0.3 remote-as 100
Router(config-router-af)# neighbor 38.0.0.3 activate
Router(config-router-af)# network 9.9.1.0 mask 255.255.255.0
Router(config-router-af)# end

Verifying VRF Configuration

There are plenty of Cisco IOS CLIs that you can use to verify an active VRF configuration.

Show ip protocols vrf <vrf-name> displays routing protocol information related to a VRF.

Show ip route vrf <vrf-name> displays IP routing table information related to a VRF.

Describe Bidirectional Forwarding Detection (BFD)

Bidirectional Forwarding Detection (or BFD) is a forwarding path failure detection method between two IP devices and can be configured for interfaces, data links and forwarding planes.

BFD (RFC 5880) uses a low overhead detection protocol that can be enabled on per-interface or per-protocol basis. BFD protocol uses a three-way handshake to establish and tear down a session between the two pre-configured devices. You can optionally configure authentication using either a simple cleartext password or MD5/SHA-1.

Protocols such as OSPF, IS-IS, BGP or even RIP can be used to start a BFD session, thus allowing these protocols to use BFD for failure detection as opposed to using their built-in keepalive based mechanisms.

BFD session can operate in asynchronous or demand modes. In asynchronous mode, both endpoints or devices send periodic hello messages to each other, and if a given number of those messages go unacknowledged, BFD will mark the given session as Down.

In demand mode, the two nodes are not required to exchange hello messages after the initial session setup for failure detection purpose. Demand mode operates on an assumption that the two endpoints have another way to verify connectivity to each other.

There are several benefits to implementing BFD as opposed to using a protocol's in-built failure detection methods (such as keepalives).

- BFD can provide <1s failure detection times out of the box which is only achievable with built-in methods with some tuning or customization.
- BFD is an standalone protocol and serves as a protocol or link independent method of failure detection.
- BFD is significantly less resource intensive because it makes use of data plane functions as opposed to control plane.

Troubleshoot EIGRP (classic and named mode)

Address families (IPv4, IPv6)

Address families (or AF) configuration harmonizes the overall routing protocol configuration regardless of the differences between IPv4 and IPv6 addressing. Cisco added support for address families in response to IPv6 adoption.

EIGRP can be configured either in classic or named mode. The classic mode is the traditional way of configuring EIGRP where EIGRP related configuration commands are found within router mode or interface modes of configuration. The named mode is a relatively newer mode of configuring EIGRP where you can configure all EIGRP commands within the router mode itself.

Named mode can contain multiple address families and autonomous systems (or ASs). There is also a vendor perspective to this feature, where for example Cisco, only added some of the newer EIGRP features only within named mode.

It is highly recommended to only configure EIGRP in named mode for all scenarios. IPv6 with VRF is only supported in named mode.

Classic Mode Configuration	Named Mode Configuration
Interface GigabitEthernet 0/0	router eigrp TEST
ipv6 enable	!
ipv6 eigrp 10	address-family ipv4 unicast
no shut	autonomous-system 10
!	!
router eigrp 10	network 0.0.0.0
eigrp router-id 20.20.20.20	eigrp router-id 20.20.20.20
network 0.0.0.0 0.0.0.0	no shutdown
	exit-address-family
ipv6 router eigrp 10	!

eigrp router-id 20.20.20.20 no shut	address-family ipv6 unicast autonomous-system 10 ! eigrp router-id 20.20.20.20 no shutdown exit-address-family

Neighbor relationship and authentication

Enhanced Interior Gateway Routing Protocol (EIGRP) is an advanced or enhanced distance vector protocol. It uses Diffused Update Algorithm (DUAL) algorithm to calculate the shortest path a destination. It is a Cisco proprietary protocol.

Once EIGRP builds neighbor relationship, it builds a topology table i.e. unlike RIP or IGRP, it doesn't rely on routing table to hold all of the information it needs to operate and then installs route from this to the routing table (much like a distance vector protocol). You can display content of topology table using show ip eigrp topology command. Topology contains both distance and vector information for each destination prefix that EIGRP knows about.

EIGRP supports authentication in order to maintain integrity of the routing updates. You can use MD5 or SHA-2 for authentication. Configuring authentication is pretty straightforward and can be done in three steps.

- Configure a key chain
- Configure a key ID and a key string.
- Choose your authentication method (MD5 or SHA-2) and finally apply authentication to your EIGRP interface(s))

Loop-free path selections (RD, FD, FC, successor, feasible successor, stuck in active)

EIGRP also establishes a specific jargon when it comes to path selection, and those terms include feasible distance, reported distance and feasible successor.

Feasible distance (or the best path or FD) is the best metric along a path to destination network. This includes the metric to the neighbor advertising the given path. Reported distance (RD) is the total metric along the path to a destination network as advertised by an upstream neighbor. Finally, a feasible successor (FC) is a path whose reported distance is less than the feasible distance.

Stubs

When Stub routing is enabled, EIGRP router (most likely Spoke device) will only advertise specific routes to the hub router, i.e. the stub router will not advertise routes received from other EIGRP neighbors back to Hub router.

There are several advantages that come with a Stub configuration.

It prevents less than optimal routing in a hub-and-spoke topology as stub spokes cannot become transit routers
With no query updates, it may help achieve faster convergence
It simplifies the router configuration

Stud routing can be configured in a variety of ways on a Cisco router. The default configuration includes connected as well as summary routes.

eigrp stub [receive-only] [leak-map name] [connected] [static] [summary] [redistributed]

- Receive-only: Strictly stub, so no outbound advertisements for any networks
- Connected: Allows advertising of directly connected networks but nothing else
- Static: Allows advertising of static routes when redistributed into EIGRP
- Summary: Allows advertising of summary routes
- Redistribute: Allows the stub router to send out routes that were distributed into EIGRP

Load balancing (equal and unequal cost)

EIGRP supports multiple equal cost paths out of the box and you can configure it using maximum-path command. Additionally, EIGRP also supports unequal cost paths load balancing which can be configured using variance command. Unequal cost paths follow the logic that any routes with a feasible distance less than 'n' times of the successor routes feasible distance can be included in the multiple paths.

Metrics

EIGRP uses minimum bandwidth and total delay to compute the routing metric. These bandwidth and delay values are what network admins have configured on the interfaces. EIGRP calculate final metric using bandwidth, delay and a set of 5 coefficients known as K values. EIGRP speaking router wouldn't form neighbor relationship with another L3 device if K values didn't match.

EIGRP metric = ([K1 * bandwidth + (K2 * bandwidth) / (256 - load) + K3 * delay] * [K5 / (reliability + K4)]) * 256

Where the default K values are K1=1, K2=0, K3=1, K4=0 and K5 = 0 which simplifies the metric formula to bandwidth plus delay.

Troubleshoot OSPF (v2/v3)

Address families (IPv4, IPv6)

The OSPFv3 enables support for address families for both IPv4 and IPv6. When used, you can have two processes per interface and one process per address family. You can configure an OSPFv3 process to be either IPv4 or IPv6.

Neighbor relationship and authentication

Open Shortest Path First (OSPF) protocol is defined in RFC 2328 and based on link-state technology where link is an interface on a L3 device such as a router. The state of the link is an attribute of that interface and its relationship to its neighbors. The interface attributes relevant to OSPF include the IP address, subnet mask, the type of the network, the routers that are also connected to that network and what have you.

Unlike distance vector protocols that use Bellman-Ford, OSPF uses shortest path first (or SPF or Dijkstra SPF) algorithm to determine the shortest to all known destination networks with the help of a graph.

When an OSPF router boots up, it generates a link-state advertisement (or LSA) for that router which represents state of links. All routers exchange their LSAs via flooding mechanism. Once exchange is completed, every router ends up with a database that is used to calculate shortest path to each destination. Each OSPF router uses Dijkstra SPF algorithm to derive shortest path tree and the result of this calculation is stored in the routing table (or RIB). The algorithm places each router at the root of a tree and then calculates the shortest path to each destination network based on the cumulate cost needed to reach that destination.

OSPF supports authentication in order to maintain integrity of the routing updates. You can use MD5 or SHA-2 for authentication. Configuring authentication is pretty straightforward and can be done in three steps.

- Configure a key chain
- Configure a key ID and a key string.
- Choose your authentication method (MD5 or SHA-2) and finally apply authentication to your OSPF interface(s)

Network types, area types, and router types

Point-to-point, multipoint, broadcast, non-broadcast

OSPF addresses three classes of network types, point to point (p2p), point to multipoint (p2mp) and broadcast.

Network Type	Default for	Configuration Requirement	Hello/Dead Timers (s)	DR/BDR Required?
Non-broadcast	FR	Static neighbors	30/120	Yes
Broadcast	Ethernet	L2 broadcast	10/40	Yes
P2p	n/a	Directly connected		No
P2mp Broadcast			30/120	No
P2mp Non-broadcast		Static neighbors, directly connected		
Loopback	Loopback	n/a	n/a	n/a

You can use "ip ospf network <type>" command to configure a network type on a per-interface basis. You can use "show ip ospf interface <interface name/number>" to verify your network type change.

Area type: backbone, normal, transit, stub, NSSA, totally stub

OSPF uses interface cost as its metric, which is inversely proportional to the bandwidth of that interface, i.e. higher bandwidth means lower cost by default unless you modify it using ip ospf cost <value> command.

Backbone is a special must-have area type that connects to all other areas (exception being a virtual link) in a given domain. It designated as 0.0.0.0 or area 0.

Normal area is any other area that connects directly (or via a virtual link) to backbone area. You can assign any number to a normal area.

Transit area is an area has a virtual link connecting two or more ABRs connected to this area. Virtual link configuration is what makes an area transit.

Stub area, as the name suggests, is an area that's isolated away from external routes from outside OSPF domain. Totally stub area is a stricter variant of stub area where no other routing information other than the given area is stored inside the LSDB.

Not-So-Stubby (or NSSA) is an area where redistributed routes use Type 7 LSAs, the LSA is generated by the NSSA's ASBR and an NSSA's ABR translates this into a Type 5 LSAs which can in turn be propagated inside the OSPF domain.

Internal router, backbone router, ABR, ASBR

Internal router is where all router's interfaces belong to a given area.

Backbone router is a router within the OSPF domain that has at least one interface connected to backbone area.

OSPF uses flooding to exchange link-state advertisements between routers and all routers within an area have exact link-state database. Routers that have interfaces in multiple areas including backbone are known as Area Border

Routers (ABRs). Routers that act as gateway between OSPF and other routing protocol or other instances of the OSPF process are known as Autonomous System Border Routers (or ASBRs). OSPF finite state machine (or FSM) includes eight different states including down, attempt, init, two-way, exstart, exchange, loading and full.

Virtual link

One of the most fundamental requirements with OSPF is that all OSPF areas must be physically (or L2 adjacent) connected to backbone area and thus preventing loop formation for the given OSPF domain. This requirement for all inter-area routing turns the entire OSPF topology into a star-like topology (or p2p). This technique is borrowed from Bellman-Ford or distance vector routing protocols where it is used to address count-to-infinity.

Now, how about a case where directly connecting an area to backbone isn't possible for example migrating another network to OSPF. In such cases, you can use virtual links across a transit area which must be directly connected to backbone area.

You can configure virtual link using "area <#> virtual-link <OSPF-router-ID>" command under the OSPF process.

Last but not least, you can also use a stock GRE tunnel between the two ABRs to achieve the to satisfy the backbone area connectivity requirement much like virtual-link, however there are some major differences between the two approaches that are worth noting. In case of GRE tunnel, the following caveats apply.

- Tunnel headers lead to more overhead (or extra bytes)
- Routing updates as well as user data traffic is tunnelled
- GRE tunnel can go through a stub area (with virtual links it has to be a non-stub transit area)

Path preference

OSPF path selection and preference criteria are pretty simple. It uses the following three ways to select the best routes (in order).

1. **Prefix length:** Longest prefix length is most preferred.
2. **Administrative Distance (AD):** If there are multiple routes to a destination with the equal prefix length, then the route learned by the protocol with the lowest AD is preferred for routing.
3. **Metric:** If there are multiple routes learned by the same protocol with same prefix length, the route with the lowest metric is preferred. However, if two or more routes have same metric values, then OSPF will ECMP.

However, OSPF path preference works out by the route type (in order) as per RFC 3101.

1. Intra-area (O)
2. Inter-area (O IA)
3. NSSA Type 1 (N1)
4. External Type 1 (E1)
5. NSSA Type 2 (N2)
6. External Type 2 (E2)

OSPF will use path preference first and then work out the best path or paths depending on the path selection criteria if needed.

Troubleshoot BGP (Internal and External)

Address families (IPv4, IPv6)

The traditional BGP only supports IPv4 unicast prefixes however MP-BGP enables support for address families for both IPv4 and IPv6 with unicast and multicast traffic types. In order to support address families, much like OSPFv3, MP-BGP differs from traditional BGP in a number of ways.

- It uses concept of Address Family Identifier (or AFI) and Sub AFI (or SAFI)
- It uses an extra attribute, MP_UNREACH_NLRI, to carry multiprotocol reachability information
- MP-BGP routers can use Capability Advertisements to announce its capabilities which a regular BGP router may either support or ignore

Neighbor relationship and authentication (next-hop, multihop, 4-byte AS, private AS, route refresh, synchronization, operation, peer group, states and timers)

BGP is an exterior gateway protocol (or EGP) so it was created from ground up to perform interdomain routing. BGP router establishes a connection using TCP to each of its neighbors. BGP router can establish two types of sessions, external or internal. If the two BGP peers reside in two different domains or autonomous systems (or ASs), the session is known as an external BGP or an eBGP session. If the two BGP peers are in the same AS, then it said to be an internal BGP or iBGP session.

By default, BGP establishes peer relationship using the IP address of the interface closest to the peering router. However, BGP peers can use neighbor update-source command to source BGP packets from another interface if so desired.

BGP next-hop-self is a well-known mandatory attribute that defines the IP address of the router that should be used as the next hop to the destinations within the UPDATE message. When a BGP router has to re-advertise an eBGP learned route via iBGP it does so without changing the next-hop. But what if the other routers do not know how to reach that next-hop? Well, there may be two ways to fix it.

1. Advertise next-hop IP subnet via an IGP, such as OSPF or EIGRP.

2. Use next-hop-self option to modify the next-hop IP address before eBGP routers send a route to iBGP speakers

Much like the shortage of IPv4 addresses, BGP 2-byte ASN (64K in total, and 63K usable) didn't last either and IANA (the responsible body) had to expand AS number space to 4-bytes thus expanding the overall possibilities from 64K to 4.2B. 4-byte support is advertised as a BGP capability within the OPEN message.

4-byte ASNs can be written in Asplain, Asdot and Asdot+ notations. Let's look at an example for each notation or format. These ASN formats are described in RFC 5396.

4-byte ASN Format	Example
Asplain (well-known format, can be used for all 4-byte ASNs)	65526 65546 4214963331
Asdot (represents first 64K ASNs)	0.65526
Asdot+ (represents ASNs after first 64K)	<high order 16-bit value in decimal>.<low order 16-bit value in decimal> 65526 = 0.65526 65546 = 1.10

BGP private ASNs range from 64512 to 64435, these ASNs are to be used by organizations worldwide without requiring an official assignment from InterNIC.

Cisco's BGP implementation comes with three route refresh options.

- Hard reset which involves bringing down the peering (clear ip bgp)
- Soft reconfiguration Inbound (makes a copy of the entire BGP table for the given neighbor before applying the policy change). It still involves bringing down the peering.

- Route Refresh Capability. BGP policy change simply results in a message to the BGP neighbor to resend all of its prefixes hence there is no impact to peering.

Route Refresh Approach	Requirements
Hard Reset	None
Soft reconfiguration	This is pretty much a hack where a local router stores unedited/unfiltered NLRI sent from a neighbor in a separate table and then processes it locally when soft reconfiguration request is made. You can configure it by using "neighbor <neighbor-address> soft-reconfiguration inbound" command under BGP router mode.
Soft Reset (Route Refresh capability) – the most preferred way.	Negotiated with an OPEN message after session setup. If supported, you can use "clear ip bgp <neighbor-address> in" to request a route refresh. You can verify support using "show ip bgp neighbors".

On Cisco IOS, Route refresh capability is also known as Dynamic Inbound Soft Reset. However, regardless of the underlying mechanics across soft reconfiguration versus soft reset, you will still need to use "clear ip bgp <neighbor-address | *> soft in" to request route refresh.

BGP synchronization rule says that if an AS provides transit to another AS, then BGP should not advertise a route until all of the routers within the given AS have learned about the route via an IGP such as OSPF or EIGRP. BGP synchronization is enabled by default.

BGP neighbors who share same outbound policies can be grouped together using a feature known as peer groups. Peer groups simplify configuration as well as reduce resource requirements for BGP routers. The scope of the feature is locally significant to the router where peer groups are configured, there are no protocol level dependencies.

BGP FSM incudes six well-known states.

- Idle
- Connect
- Active
- OpenSent
- OpenConfirm
- Established

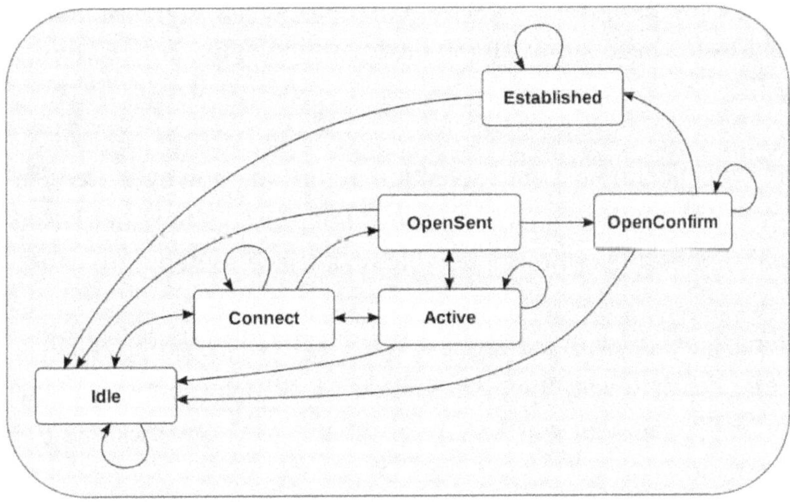

BGP uses both keepalive and hold-down timers. By default, on Cisco routers, keepalive timer is set to 60 seconds whereas hold-down timer is 3x or 300% of keepalive value or 180 seconds long. Juniper routers implement a more aggressive set of these timers where keepalive and hold-down are set to 30 seconds and 90 seconds respectively.

You can display current keepalive and hold-time interval values using "show ip bgp neighbors" command.

Beyond the two most basic timers of keepalive and hold-down, BGP protocol uses a bunch of other timers for various purposes.

- Advertisement Timer
- Scan Timer

Path preference (attributes and best-path)

BGP routers can receive multiple paths to the same destination but BGP router uses best path selection algorithm and would only install the best route in the routing table. BGP assigns the first valid path as the current best path, but then BGP compares the best path with the next path in the list until BGP reaches the end of the list.

Here is the sequence of best path selection algorithm, however, keep in mind that a lot of these tests can be overridden or even bypassed altogether based on the various BGP knobs and options available on a Cisco router.

1. Prefer the path with the highest WEIGHT (Cisco proprietary)
2. Prefer the path with the highest LOCAL_PREF (default value is 100)
3. Prefer the path that was locally originated via network or aggregate commands
4. Prefer the path with the shortest AS_PATH
5. Prefer the path with the lowest origin type
6. Prefer the path with the lowest MED
7. Prefer eBGP over iBGP
8. Prefer the path with the lowest IGP metric to the BGP next hop (best path is already selected at this point)
9. Optionally, if BGP Multipath is configured, then continue further.

a. When two best paths exist, prefer the path that was received first (the older one)
b. Prefer the route that comes from the BGP router with the lowest router ID
c. If the originator or the router ID is same for multiple paths, prefer the path with the minimum cluster list length
d. Prefer the path that comes from the lowest neighbor address

Route reflector (excluding multiple route reflectors, confederations, dynamic peer)

The iBGP routers need to be connected in a full-mesh configuration because BGP doesn't allow iBGP routers to re-advertise routes learned via iBGP speakers to other iBGP peers. This loop prevention requirement doesn't exist for eBGP peers since they rely on AS Path to perform similar function.

Going by the full-mesh requirement, if you have n peers in an iBGP full-mesh, you'd have n-1 peering relationships which is very difficult to scale due to resource requirements. BGP provides two approaches to go around the iBGP full-mesh requirement.

- Route reflectors
- Confederations

A BGP route reflector is an iBGP speaker that reflects routes learned from other iBGP peers to its other peers. Route reflector client is an iBGP router that receives and sends out routes to other iBGP speakers by way of reflection. Router reflector client routers do not need to maintain a full mesh with other clients.

BGP confederations is another way to scale iBGP. The idea is logically divide an AS into multiple sub-ASs, the routers outside the confederation only see the confederation AS. iBGP peers that reside in a given sub-AS are known as internal peers, whereas the ones in different sub-ASs are considered external peers.

Routing advertisements with confederation work similarly to how they do with route reflector setup. The simplest way to understand confederations is that iBGP peering between sub-AS function like eBGP.

BGP dynamic neighbor feature allows BGP peering to a group of neighbors that are defined by pre-configuring a range of IP addresses. Effectively, the IP address range acts like a block of IP addresses that BGP listens on to establish future peering. Once configured, and as soon as a TCP session is initiated by a remote router, the router configured with dynamic neighbor with the remote IP address, dynamically creates a peering relationship.

Policies (inbound/outbound filtering, path manipulation)

BGP allows granular route filtering mechanism in the form of BGP Outbound Route Filtering (ORF). BGP ORF uses send and receive capabilities advertised to the peer routers. When received by the peer, it conveys that the router will accept a prefix list from this neighbor and apply the prefix list to locally configured ORFs. This allows an eBGP speaker to install the inbound prefix list filter to the remote peer as an outbound filter.
BGP ORF requires that BGP peering ORF capabilities are enabled on each participating peer router before prefix based ORF announcements can be received.

Sending Router (Local, say a CE router)

```
ip prefix-list ACCEPTABLE-ROUTES seq 5 permit 0.0.0.0/0
ip prefix-list ACCEPTABLE-ROUTES seq 10 permit 12.0.0/8
ip prefix-list ACCEPTABLE-ROUTES seq 15 permit 15.0.0.0/8

neighbor <remote-PE-peer> capability orf prefix-list send
neighbor <remote-PE-peer> prefix-list ACCEPTABLE-ROUTES in
```

neighbor <CE-peer> capability orf prefix-list receive

If the session was already established between the two routers, you'll need to issue "clear ip bgp in prefix-filter" command before ORF takes effect. In order to verify your configuration, you can use "show ip bgp neighbors <remote-peer> received prefix-filter" command.

```
CE# sh ip bgp neighbors 192.1.1.1 received prefix-filter
Address family: IPv4 Unicast
ip prefix-list 192.1.1.1: 4 entries
   seq 5 permit 0.0.0.0/0
   seq 10 permit 12.0.0.0/8
   seq 15 permit 15.0.0.0/8
```

BGP ORF prefix-based filtering also works in a cross-vendor setup, e.g. when connecting a Cisco CE router to a Juniper's PE or SP router.

BGP supports path manipulation or traffic engineering in a variety of ways. In the BGP world, there are only two possibilities, i.e. path manipulation for Outbound or Inbound traffic.

Outbound Path Manipulation

Local preference can be used to perform outbound path manipulation as BGP uses path with the highest Local Preference. Local preference attribute is never sent out of the AS (not advertised to eBGP peers) so it is only locally significant.

Weight is another attribute that can be used to manipulate outbound traffic however it is even more restricted in its scope than Local Preference – it is only locally significant to the router where it is configured and is never sent out to either iBGP or eBGP neighbors.

For inbound traffic manipulation, you can use lower MED to inbound traffic engineering but if the remote router or routers have higher Local Preference attribute configured, which happens to more preferred in the BGP path selection criteria, there is no chance that manipulating MED will help steer traffic over a path into your AS.

AS Path Prepending is another way to potentially influence traffic coming into your AS, trick is to simply make AS-PATH longer by prepending your own AS number when sending out eBGP updates to your undesired upstream router(s) or providers. Once you prepend an AS path, it is likely but not guaranteed that your AS is not used for inbound traffic from those undesired providers.

You can also use BGP conditional advertisements and BGP communities for relatively more complex path manipulation.

Chapter 2 VPN Technologies

This chapter covers the following exam topics from Cisco's official Enterprise Advanced Routing and Services (ENARSI) 300-410 V1.0 exam blueprint.

- Describe MPLS operations (LSR, LDP, label switching, LSP)
- Describe MPLS Layer 3 VPN
- Configure and verify DMVPN (single hub)
  - GRE/mGRE
  - NHRP
  - IPsec
  - Dynamic neighbor
  - Spoke-to-spoke

Describe MPLS operations (LSR, LDP, label switching, LSP)

MPLS is an encapsulation technique that help facilitate delivery of IP services. It uses labels that are appended to frames or packets. It supports a wide variety of layer 2 technologies such as Ethernet, Packet over SONET, PPP, FR and ATM. MPLS is sometimes called layer 2.5 protocol simply to convey the fact that it inherits characteristics from both layer 2 (e.g. forwarding paths) and layer 3 (e.g. ability to use signaling mechanisms) protocols.

MPLS label header is 32-bit long where 20 bits represent the actual MPLS label, 3 bits are allocated for COS/EXP, 1 bit to indicate Bottom of Stack and finally 8 bits for TTL. The actual placement of label depends on the underlying medium but generally it is placed between the L2 headers and the L2/L3 packet. MPLS doesn't forward packets hop-by-hop unlike IP, instead it uses a concept of path which is established for a source/destination pair. In MPLS jargon, these paths are known as Label Switched Paths (or LSPs).

Forwarding Equivalence Class (or FEC) determines how packets are mapped to LSP, so these are set of packets with similar characteristics (e.g. an IP prefix) which are forwarded the way same way using the same LSP.

Label Switched Router (or LSR) is an MPLS router that switches data traffic using MPLS labels. Label Distribution Protocol (or LDP) enables LSRs in an MPLS network to exchange label binding information. LDP enables LSRs to request, distribute, and release label prefix binding information to peer routers in an MPLS network. LSRs can be located at the ingress, egress or inside the MPLS network or cloud.

The MPLS includes multiple label operations which include swap, push and pop. LSR figures out which label operation to use and what the next hop is to which the packet needs to be forwarded to. The swap operation simply means that the LSR swaps the top label in the label switch with another, whereas push operation means that the top label is replaced with another and then one or more labels are pushed onto the label stack. Finally, the pop operation means that the top label is removed altogether.

Label lookup is different than IP lookup. When a router receives a labeled packet, the lookup is done inside a known as the LFIB. If the packet is forwarded using the LFIB then it is forwarded as a label packet, on the other hand if the LSR uses CEF table to complete the forwarding then the packet leaves the LSR unlabeled (or as an IP packet) typically the case at the egress LSR. You can lookup LFIB table using "show mpls forwarding-table" command.

Describe MPLS Layer 3 VPN

Virtual Private Network (or VPN) is a solution where multiple sites can connect and communicate privately over a public infrastructure. MPLS L3 VPNs operate as an MPLS application and a collection of sites that connect via an MPLS SP core network. Each customer site is connected by way of one or more customer edge (CE) devices and likewise each provider's point of presence is connected by way of one or more provider edge (PE) device. There is also a Provider (P) device which carries out MPLS switching without regard to VPN labels.

There are three major components of an MPLS VPN network.

- VPN route target (RT) communities: RTs are used to control the import and export of routes among and to the other VRFs. Technically, it takes form of an extended BGP community. It is not be confused with route distinguisher (RD) which is a way of distinguishing overlapping routing information across VRFs. It is simply a 64-bit number that is carried along with a route via MP-BGP.
- MP-BGP: Multiprotocol-BGP is the protocol that is used to communicate VRF reachability information to all members of a VPN, hence MP-BGP must be configured on all PE devices.

- MPLS switching or forwarding: MPLS is used to transport the VPN traffic across an SP core network.

Let's now deeply look at the functions that a PE router performs in an MPLS VPN topology. PE router performs the following functions.

- It exchanges routing information with CE device
- It translates CE routing information into VPNv4 routes
- It exchanges VPNv4 routes with other PE devices using MP-BGP

MPLS VPNs can also be configured as an OSI layer 2 service.

Configure and verify DMVPN (single hub)

Dynamic Multipoint VPN (or DMVPN) is a Cisco proprietary solution for building scalable and secure IPsec/GRE based VPN tunnels. DMVPN is based on hub and spoke topologies which also allows for direct spoke to spoke communication. It provides simplified branch configuration and where adding new branches do not require changes on DMVPN Hub device(s).

Cisco rolled out DMVPN solutions in several so-called phases.

DMVPN Phase	Supported Topologies	Routing Design	Control Plane	Data Plane
1		Limited, no multicast between Spokes	Control channel traffic flows via Hub	Spoke to Spoke traffic flows via Hub
2	Spoke to Hub and Spoke to Spoke			Spoke to
3		Any IGP can be used, scalable	NHRP redirect and shortcut support	Spoke traffic flows directly without hair pinning at the Hub

DMVPN can be implemented in many ways, including the following topology variations.

- Single DMVPN Cloud, Single Tier Hub
- Single DMVPN Cloud, Dual Tier Hub
- Dual DMVPN Cloud, Single Tier Hub
- Dual DMVPN Cloud, Dual Tier Hub

While hardly ever deployed, DMVPN solution can be implemented without IPSec encryption. Tier refers to the fact whether separation of GRE encapsulation and IPSec encryption functions is implemented or not. Single tier refers to both functions collapsed onto a single router and dual tier alludes to a setup where the two functions are physically separated to two devices.

However, in all DMVPN topologies and for all practical purposes, you will still need to configure the following solution components.

- Next-Hop Resolution Protocol (or NHRP)
- mGRE Tunnels
- IPSec encryption (Tunnel Protection)

NHRP is an IETF ratified client and server protocol where Hub assumes a server role while the Spokes take on the client roles. DMVPN hub maintains an NHRP database which includes WAN overlay (or public) address of each spoke. Each spoke needs to register its public IP address when it boots up and queries the NHRP database for destination spokes to build direct tunnels.

Multipoint GRE allows a single GRE interface to support multiple IPsec tunnels and simplifies the size of the configuration. Spoke to spoke tunnels are established when there is some interesting traffic to serve as a trigger. Once spoke to spoke tunnels are up despite lack of traffic until a preconfigured amount of inactivity.

Day in the Life of DMVPN

- Each spoke maintains a permanent IPsec tunnel to the DMVPN hub, whereas spoke to spoke tunnels are brought up on demand.
- When a spoke needs to send traffic to another spoke, i.e. traffic originating from the network or subnet behind the spoke to a destination network or subnet behind another spoke, the spoke would query NHRP server or Hub for destination spoke's public IP address.
- Once a spoke receives information on destination Spoke's public IP address, it attempts to initiate a dynamic IPsec tunnel to it.
- This spoke to spoke tunnel is built over the mGRE interface
- In the current DMVPN solution (or Phase 3), spokes can simply bypass the Hub and use spoke to spoke GRE/IPsec tunnel instead.

Single DMVPN Cloud, Single Tier Hub

This is the simplest form of DMVPN deployment. It consists of a single DMVPN hub located typically at the organization's HQ whereas multiple spokes can be located anywhere in the form of branch offices.

Single tier refers to the fact that all control planes are collapsed onto single router, i.e. Hub and it runs NHRP, mGRE and IPsec features. As we discussed earlier, the hub maintains the NHRP database and keeps tracks of each Spoke's public IP address. DMVPN Hub can be behind a static NAT device whereas Spoke routers can be behind a static NAT or even a PAT device. Two spokes that are behind PAT devices can't build up direct spoke to spoke tunnels for communication so traffic in that case must traverse the Hub router.

This kind of DMVPN topology where all control plane activities are converged at the Hub router requires more resources than a typical Spoke router. With single tier DMVPN, you can use dynamic routing protocol or simply go with static routes.

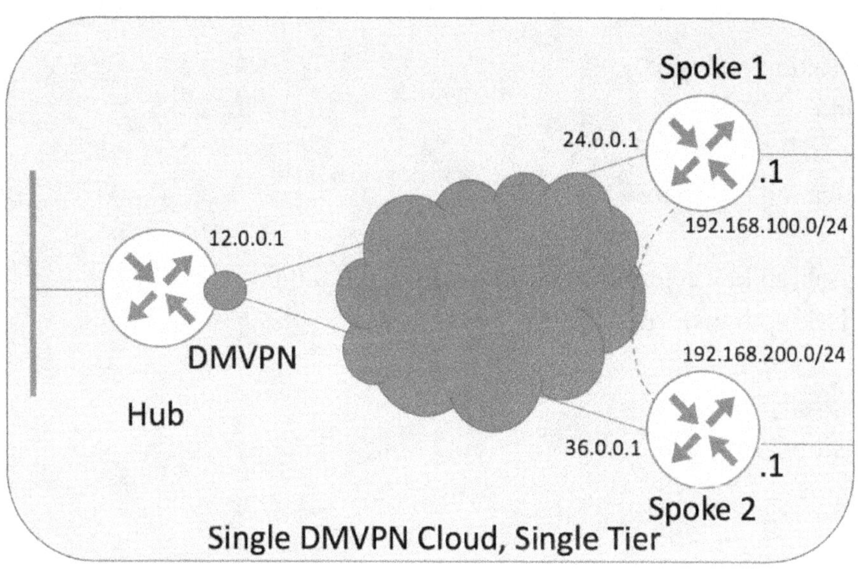

DMVPN Hub Configuration

```
interface gi0/0
ip address 12.0.0.1 255.0.0.0
no shut

ip route 192.168.100.0 255.255.255.0 12.0.0.2
ip route 192.168.200.0 255.255.255.0 12.0.0.2


interface tunnel0
ip address 10.1.1.1 255.255.255.0
ip nhrp map multicast dynamic
ip nhrp network-id 100
ip nhrp redirect
ip nhrp shortcut
tunnel source 12.0.0.1
tunnel mode gre multipoint
ip mtu 1416
tunnel protection ipsec profile DMVPN
```

```
crypto isakmp policy 10
hash md5
encryption 3des
authentication pre-share

crypto isakmp key cciein8weeks address 0.0.0.0 0.0.0.0
crypto isakmp transform CC8 esp-3des

crypto ipsec profile DMVPN
set transform-set CC8
```

DMVPN Spoke 1 Configuration

```
interface gi0/0
ip address 24.0.0.1 255.0.0.0
no shut

ip route 12.0.0.1 255.255.255.255 24.0.0.2

interface gi0/1
ip address 192.168.100.1 255.255.255.0
no shut

interface tunnel0
ip address 10.1.1.2 255.255.255.0
ip nhrp map 10.1.1.1 12.0.0.1
ip nhrp network-id 100
ip nhrp nhs 10.1.1.1
ip nhrp shortcut
tunnel source 24.0.0.1
tunnel mode gre multipoint
ip mtu 1416
```

tunnel protection ipsec profile DMVPN

crypto isakmp policy 10
hash md5
encryption 3des
authentication pre-share

crypto isakmp key cciein8weeks address 0.0.0.0 0.0.0.0
crypto isakmp transform CC8 esp-3des

crypto ipsec profile DMVPN
set transform-set CC8

DMVPN Spoke 2 Configuration

interface gi0/0
ip address 36.0.0.1 255.0.0.0
no shut

ip route 12.0.0.1 255.255.255.255 36.0.0.2

interface gi0/1
ip address 192.168.200.1 255.255.255.0
no shut

interface tunnel0
ip address 10.1.1.3 255.255.255.0
ip nhrp map 10.1.1.1 12.0.0.1
ip nhrp map multicast 12.0.0.1
ip nhrp network-id 100
ip nhrp nhs 10.1.1.1
ip nhrp shortcut
tunnel source 36.0.0.1

tunnel mode gre multipoint
ip mtu 1416
tunnel protection ipsec profile DMVPN

crypto isakmp policy 10
hash md5
encryption 3des
authentication pre-share

crypto isakmp key cciein8weeks address 0.0.0.0 0.0.0.0
crypto isakmp transform CC8 esp-3des

crypto ipsec profile DMVPN
set transform-set CC8

ip route 12.0.0.1 255.255.255.255 36.0.0.2

Verification

You can verify DMVPN configuration by sending packets behind any of the spoke and or using "show dmvpn" command.

Single DMVPN Cloud, Dual Tier Hub

This is a slightly complex variation of single DMVPN cloud and single tier where mGRE and IPsec functions are separated two routers on the Hub side. This separation of functions provides more resources or headroom for control plane functions while the first-tier router offloads all IPSec functions.

Due to separation of control plane from the data plane, spoke to spoke direct connections are not possible in this setup.

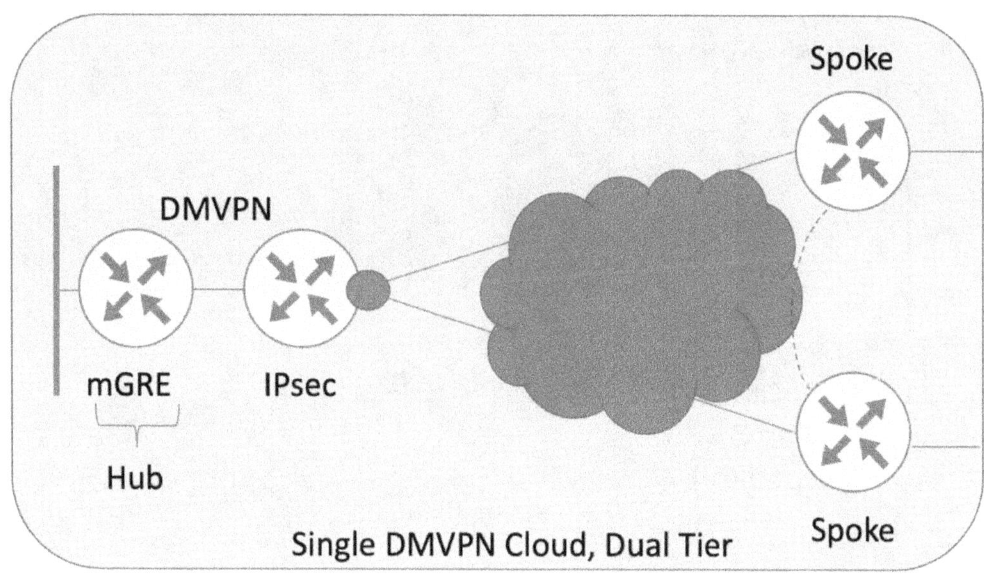

Dual DMVPN Cloud, Single Tier Hub

Dual DMVPN refers to two Hub routers where each router performs DMVPN control and data plane functions combined into one device. One Hub is used as primary whereas the other is used as secondary or backup.

This is a scalable and flexible variation of DMVPN deployment, it provides redundancy while still supporting dynamic spoke to spoke tunnels as long as both source and destination networks and corresponding spoke tunnels are terminated on the same DMVPN cloud.

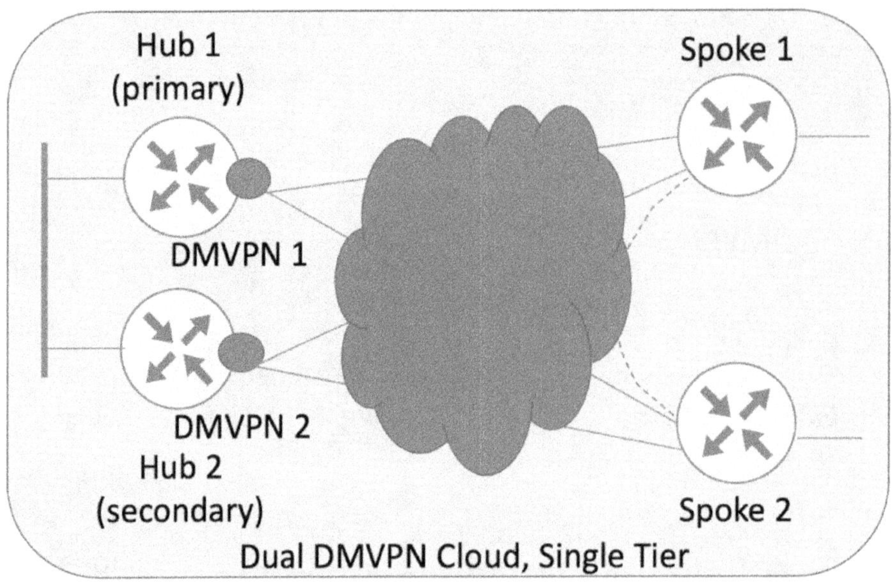

Dual DMVPN Cloud, Dual Tier Hub

Dual DMVPN with dual tier (much like single DMVPN dual tier) separates out the DMVPN control plane and data plane functions resulting in higher scales along with node-level redundancy.

All dual tier designs suffer from the limitations of no direct spoke to spoke tunnels due to separation of planes as mentioned earlier.

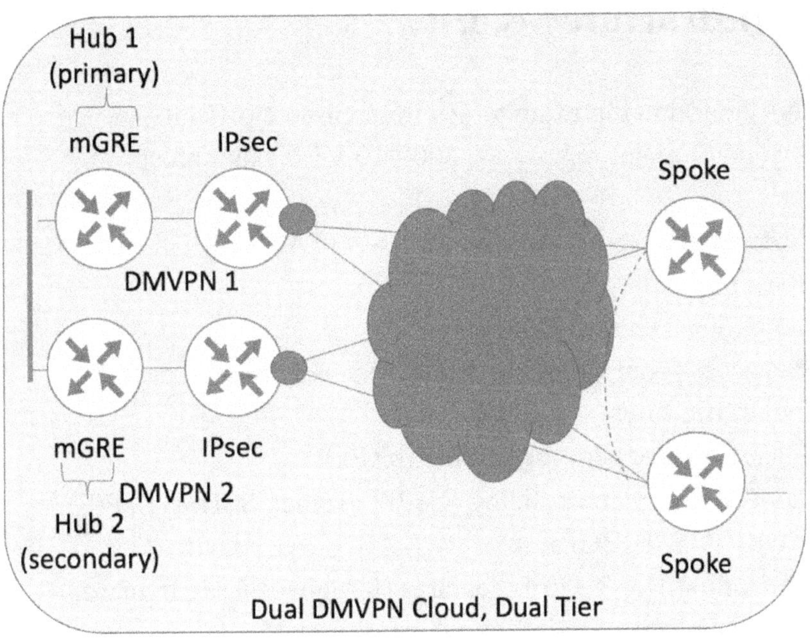

Hub 1
(primary)
mGRE
IPsec
DMVPN 1
mGRE
IPsec
DMVPN 2
Hub 2
(secondary)
Spoke
Spoke
Dual DMVPN Cloud, Dual Tier

Chapter 3 Infrastructure Security

This chapter covers the following exam topics from Cisco's official Enterprise Advanced Routing and Services (ENARSI) 300-410 V1.0 exam blueprint.

- Troubleshoot device security using IOS AAA (TACACS+, RADIUS, local database)
- Troubleshoot router security features
    - IPv4 access control lists (standard, extended, time-based)
    - IPv6 traffic filter
    - Unicast reverse path forwarding (uRPF)
- Troubleshoot control plane policing (CoPP) (Telnet, SSH, HTTP(S), SNMP, EIGRP, OSPF, BGP)
- Describe IPv6 First Hop security features (RA guard, DHCP guard, binding table, ND inspection/snooping, source guard)

Troubleshoot device security using IOS AAA (TACACS+, RADIUS, local database)

One of the fundamentals aspect of securing network infrastructure is to use passwords protection to control and restrict access to the device CLI. Command line or what Cisco calls EXEC access to a router can be made in several ways however all connections inbound into a router come in via TTY line.

There are four types of TTY lines, you can display what's supported on your device by using show line command.

1. CTY
2. TTY
3. AUX
4. VTY

CTY is your console port. On any router, it appears in the router configuration as line con <#>. TTY lines are asynchronous lines used for inbound and outbound remote access either via a modem or terminal connection. It is referred to as line <#> on a router. AUX is auxiliary port and you can spot within the configuration as line aux <#>. VTY lines are virtual terminal lines of a router and are used primarily to control inbound telnet or SSH connections. You can configure them by using line vty 0 <#> command.

Configuring a password on a line is straightforward. You must go into enable mode, followed by line mode and then configure the password.

```
router#configure terminal
Enter configuration commands, one per line.  End with CNTL/Z.
router(config)#line con 0
router(config-line)#password cciein8weeks
router(config-line)#login
```

If you want to configure local user specific password, all you need to do is to add username and password pairs and turn on local authentication using login local command.

```
router#configure terminal
        Enter configuration commands, one per line.  End with CNTL/Z.
        router(config)#username user1 password password1
        router(config)#username user2 password password2
        router(config)#username user3 password password3
router(config)#line vty 0 4
router(config-line)#login local
```

Authentication and authorization using AAA

To enable authentication, authorization, and accounting (AAA) authentication for line logins, you can use the login authentication command in line configuration mode. You also need to configure AAA services.

Let's now configure user authentication via TACACS+.

```
router#configure terminal
Enter configuration commands, one per line.  End with CNTL/Z.
router(config)#aaa new-model
router(config)#aaa authentication login my-auth-list tacacs+
router(config)#tacacs-server host 192.168.1.101
router(config)#tacacs-server key cciein8weeks
router(config)#line 1 8
router(config-line)#login authentication my-auth-list
```

Troubleshoot router security features

IPv4 access control lists (standard, extended, time-based)

Access lists (or ACLs) are stateless L2-L4 packet filters to specify what should be permitted and denied inbound or outbound to and from a network. As a reference, firewalls are stateful packet filters and can operate from L2 to L7 packet headers or data.

ACLs configuration requires three pieces of information, i.e.

1. Network or IP address (to be permitted or blocked)
2. Reverse mask (for ease of configuration)
3. Direction (inbound or outbound or both)

ACL Configuration

```
router#configure terminal
Enter configuration commands, one per line.  End with CNTL/Z.
router(config)#access-list 101 deny icmp any any
router(config)#access-list 101 permit ip any any
router(config)#^Z


router#configure terminal
Enter configuration commands, one per line.  End with CNTL/Z.
router(config)#no access-list 101 deny icmp any any
router(config)#^Z

router#show access-list
router#
 *Mar  9 00:43:29.832: %SYS-5-CONFIG_I: Configured from console by
console
```

ACL Verification

```
router#show access-list
Extended IP access list 101
```

```
    deny icmp any any
    permit ip any any
router#
```

Further Reading

ACL Configuration Guide

IPv6 Traffic Filter

IPv6 packet filtering is similar to standard IPv4 ACLs. IPv6 ACLs can be constructed much like IPv4 ACLs that include permit and deny statements. IPv6 extended ACLs, like their IPv4 counterpart, extend functionality offered by IPv6 standard ACLs with options such as filtering based on IPv6 option headers and upper layer protocols.

```
ipv6 access-list CCIEin8Weeks
permit tcp 2001:DB8:0400:0001::/32 eq telnet any
deny tcp host 2001:CB8:2::2 any log-input

interface giga 0/0
ipv6 traffic-filter CCIEin8Weeks out
```

You can verify an IPv6 ACL configuration using "show ipv6 access-list" command.

```
Router> show ipv6 access-list

IPv6 access list inbound
    permit ip any any eq eigrp (120 matches) sequence 5
    permit tcp any any eq ssh (150 matches) sequence 10
    permit udp any any  sequence 30
```

Further Reading

IPv6 Packet Filter

Unicast reverse path forwarding (uRPF)

Unicast Reverse Path Forwarding (uRPF) is a security feature that allows verifying reachability of the source IP address in packets being forwarded out. In essence, it helps protect the network infrastructure and users against spoofing attack.

RPF checks are a norm in multicast routing since multicast routing doesn't accept or forward incoming packets unless they are received on an interface that is the outgoing interface (OIL) for unicast route to the source of each of the packet. This technique is used to avoid routing loops and packet duplication in multicast networks.

Now, unicast routing can be configured in three different modes, i.e.

1. Strict mode
2. Loose mode
3. VRF mode

In strict mode uRPF, the packet must be received on the interface that the router would use to forward it back to the source. It means that strict mode may drop a legit packet in a typical scenario such as asymmetric routing configuration.

In loose mode uRPF, the packet source address must be in the routing table however it can be further relaxed with "allow-default" option which allows for the use of default route as part of the source verification process.

Regardless of the mode, uRPF configuration can be accomplished with one command line.

interface giga 0/0
ip verify unicast source reachable-via {rx | any} [allow-default] [allow-self-ping] [list]

You can troubleshoot and verify uRPF configuration using "show cef interface <intf-name>" command.

router#show cef interface giga 0/0
GigabitEthernet0/0 is up (if_number 4)
Corresponding hwidb fast_if_number 4
Corresponding hwidb firstsw->if_number 4
Internet address is 12.0.0.1/8
ICMP redirects are always sent
Per packet load-sharing is disabled
IP unicast RPF check is enabled
Inbound access list is not set
Outbound access list is not set
Hardware idb is GigabitEthernet0/0
IP CEF switching enabled
IP CEF Fast switching turbo vector
Input fast flags 0x0, Input fast flags2 0x0, Output fast flags 0x0, Output fast flags2 0x0
ifindex 1(1)
IP MTU 1500

Troubleshoot control plane policing (CoPP) (Telnet, SSH, HTTP(S), SNMP, EIGRP, OSPF, BGP)

You can divide a networking device into four distinct logical groups as far as traffic to/from or through a device is concerned.

1. Data plane (traffic that is not sourced or destined from/to the device, i.e. transit traffic)

2. Control plane (traffic sourced or destined from/to the device, traffic type used for the creation and operation of the network such as BGP, OSPF and ARP)
3. Management plane (technically same as control plane traffic but for the purpose of network management such as TFTP, SSH, SNMP, FTP, NTP etc.)
4. Services plane (a special case of data plane traffic but in this case, router is involved in modifying the packet header or payload, such as GRE, QoS, NAT etc.)

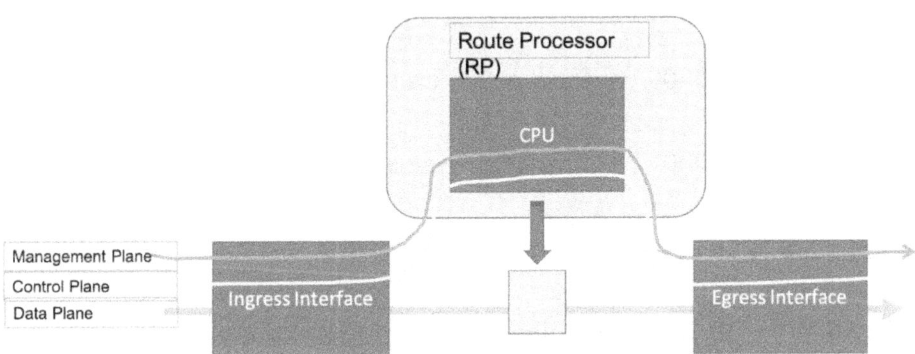

CoPP is the router processor protection mechanism, so it applies to all packets that get punted to the router processor. CoPP is about protecting the punt path, not just the control plane.

You can implement CoPP using the modular QoS CLI.

Router#show running-config
Building configuration...

.

. ---<skip>---
!
class-map match-all Catch-All-IP
 match access-group 124

```
class-map match-all Management
 match access-group 121
class-map match-all Normal
 match access-group 122
class-map match-all Undesirable
 match access-group 123
class-map match-all Routing
 match access-group 120
!
policy-map CCIEin8Weeks_CoPP
 class Undesirable
 police 8000 1500 1500 conform-action drop exceed-action drop
 class Routing
 police 1000000 50000 50000 conform-action transmit exceed-action transmit
 class Management
 police 100000 20000 20000 conform-action transmit exceed-action drop
 class Normal
 police 50000 5000 5000 conform-action transmit exceed-action drop
 class Catch-All-IP
 police 50000 5000 5000 conform-action transmit exceed-action drop
 class class-default
 police 8000 1500 1500 conform-action transmit exceed-action transmit
!
access-list 120 permit tcp any gt 1024 10.0.1.0 0.0.0.255 eq bgp
access-list 120 permit tcp any eq bgp 10.0.1.0 0.0.0.255 gt 1024 established
access-list 120 permit tcp any gt 1024 10.0.1.0 0.0.0.255 eq 639
access-list 120 permit tcp any eq 639 10.0.1.0 0.0.0.255 gt 1024 established
access-list 120 permit tcp any 10.0.1.0 0.0.0.255 eq 646
access-list 120 permit udp any 10.0.1.0 0.0.0.255 eq 646
access-list 120 permit ospf any 10.0.1.0 0.0.0.255
access-list 120 permit ospf any host 224.0.0.5
access-list 120 permit ospf any host 224.0.0.6
access-list 120 permit eigrp any 10.0.1.0 0.0.0.255
access-list 120 permit eigrp any host 224.0.0.10
```

access-list 121 permit tcp 10.0.2.0 0.0.0.255 10.0.1.0 0.0.0.255 eq telnet
access-list 121 permit tcp 10.0.2.0 0.0.0.255 eq telnet 10.0.1.0 0.0.0.255 established
access-list 121 permit tcp 10.0.2.0 0.0.0.255 10.0.1.0 0.0.0.255 eq 22
access-list 121 permit tcp 10.0.2.0 0.0.0.255 eq 22 10.0.1.0 0.0.0.255 established
access-list 121 permit udp 10.0.2.0 0.0.0.255 10.0.1.0 0.0.0.255 eq snmp
access-list 121 permit tcp 10.0.2.0 0.0.0.255 10.0.1.0 0.0.0.255 eq www
access-list 121 permit udp 10.0.2.0 0.0.0.255 10.0.1.0 0.0.0.255 eq 443
access-list 121 permit tcp 10.0.2.0 0.0.0.255 10.0.1.0 0.0.0.255 eq ftp
access-list 121 permit tcp 10.0.2.0 0.0.0.255 10.0.1.0 0.0.0.255 eq ftp-data
access-list 121 permit udp 10.0.2.0 0.0.0.255 10.0.1.0 0.0.0.255 eq syslog
access-list 121 permit udp 10.0.3.0 0.0.0.255 eq domain 10.0.1.0 0.0.0.255
access-list 121 permit udp 10.0.4.0 0.0.0.255 10.0.1.0 0.0.0.255 eq ntp
access-list 122 permit icmp any 10.0.1.0 0.0.0.255 echo
access-list 122 permit icmp any 10.0.1.0 0.0.0.255 echo-reply
access-list 122 permit icmp any 10.0.1.0 0.0.0.255 ttl-exceeded
access-list 122 permit icmp any 10.0.1.0 0.0.0.255 packet-too-big
access-list 122 permit icmp any 10.0.1.0 0.0.0.255 port-unreachable
access-list 122 permit icmp any 10.0.1.0 0.0.0.255 unreachable
access-list 122 permit pim any any
access-list 122 permit udp any any eq pim-auto-rp
access-list 122 permit igmp any any
access-list 122 permit gre any any
access-list 123 permit icmp any any fragments
access-list 123 permit udp any any fragments
access-list 123 permit tcp any any fragments
access-list 123 permit ip any any fragments
access-list 123 permit udp any any eq 1434
access-list 123 permit tcp any any eq 639 rst
access-list 123 permit tcp any any eq bgp rst
access-list 124 permit tcp any any
access-list 124 permit udp any any
access-list 124 permit icmp any any
access-list 124 permit ip any any

```
!
control-plane
 service-policy input CCIEin8Weeks_CoPP
!
```

You can verify CoPP configuration by using the show policy-map control-plane command.

```
Router#show policy-map control-plane
 Control Plane
 Service-policy input: CCIEin8Weeks_CoPP
 Class-map: Undesirable (match-all)
 0 packets, 0 bytes
 5 minute offered rate 0 bps, drop rate 0 bps
 Match: access-group 123
 police:
  cir 8000 bps, bc 1500 bytes
 conformed 0 packets, 0 bytes; actions:
  drop
 exceeded 0 packets, 0 bytes; actions:
  drop
 conformed 0 bps, exceed 0 bps
 Class-map: Routing (match-all)
 0 packets, 0 bytes
 5 minute offered rate 0 bps, drop rate 0 bps
 Match: access-group 120
 police:
  cir 1000000 bps, bc 50000 bytes
 conformed 0 packets, 0 bytes; actions:
  transmit
 exceeded 0 packets, 0 bytes; actions:
  transmit
 conformed 0 bps, exceed 0 bps
 Class-map: Management (match-all)
```

0 packets, 0 bytes
5 minute offered rate 0 bps, drop rate 0 bps
Match: access-group 121
police:
 cir 100000 bps, bc 20000 bytes
conformed 0 packets, 0 bytes; actions:
 transmit
exceeded 0 packets, 0 bytes; actions:
 drop
conformed 0 bps, exceed 0 bps
Class-map: Normal (match-all)
0 packets, 0 bytes
5 minute offered rate 0 bps, drop rate 0 bps
Match: access-group 122
police:
 cir 50000 bps, bc 5000 bytes
conformed 0 packets, 0 bytes; actions:
 transmit
exceeded 0 packets, 0 bytes; actions:
 drop
conformed 0 bps, exceed 0 bps
Class-map: Catch-All-IP (match-all)
50461 packets, 24038351 bytes
5 minute offered rate 4000 bps, drop rate 0 bps
Match: access-group 124
police:
 cir 50000 bps, bc 5000 bytes
conformed 50444 packets, 24031001 bytes; actions:
 transmit
exceeded 17 packets, 7350 bytes; actions:
 drop
conformed 4000 bps, exceed 0 bps
Class-map: class-default (match-any)
16785 packets, 1183331 bytes

```
5 minute offered rate 0 bps, drop rate 0 bps
Match: any
police:
 cir 8000 bps, bc 1500 bytes
conformed 16658 packets, 1175711 bytes; actions:
 transmit
exceeded 127 packets, 7620 bytes; actions:
 transmit
 conformed 0 bps, exceed 0 bps
Router#
```

Describe IPv6 First Hop security features (RA guard, DHCP guard, binding table, ND inspection/snooping, source guard)

IPv6 First Hope Security (or FHS) features help implement IPv6 security over the L2 links. These are configured on a Cisco switch that sits between the end stations and the first-hop router.

FHS features include the following.

- IPv6 snooping
- IPv6 Router Advertisement Guard (RA Guard)
- IPv6 Destination Guard
- IPv6 Source Guard
- IPv6 Prefix Guard
- Binding Table Recovery
- Data gleaning

IPv6 snooping combines several security features into one. It includes IPv6 Neighbor Discovery (ND) inspection, IPv6 device tracking, IPv6 address glean, and IPv6 binding table recovery.

Router Advertisements (RAs) are used by IPv6 devices to announce themselves on the link. IPv6 RA feature allows network engineers to block unwanted RA guard messages. It can be configured in host or router mode. In host mode, all RA and router direct messages are filtered out on the port. The RA guard feature compares what's configured on the switch (or L2 device) with what's found inside the RA and router redirect frames, the frame is forwarded if the contents are validated otherwise it is dropped.

IPv6 source guard uses IPv6 ND inspection or IPv6 address glean to deny or drop data traffic when it is originated from an address that's not found within the binding table. IPv6 source guard can help deny traffic from unknown or unallocated sources. IPv6 destination guard feature uses IPv6 ND process to ensure that the device only performs IPv6 address resolution only for those addresses that are known or expected to be active on the link.

IPv6 prefix guard feature goes hand in hand with the IPv6 source guard feature to allow a device to deny traffic that originated from say outside the scope that's allocated by the DHCP. It uses prefix glean in RA and prefix delegation or even static configuration.

Chapter 4 Infrastructure Services

This chapter covers the following exam topics from Cisco's official Enterprise Advanced Routing and Services (ENARSI) 300-410 V1.0 exam blueprint.

- Troubleshoot device management
    - Console and VTY
    - Telnet, HTTP, HTTPS, SSH, SCP
    - (T)FTP
- Troubleshoot SNMP (v2c, v3)
- Troubleshoot network problems using logging (local, syslog, debugs, conditional debugs, timestamps)
- Troubleshoot IPv4 and IPv6 DHCP (DHCP client, IOS DHCP server, DHCP relay, DHCP options)
- Troubleshoot network performance issues using IP SLA (jitter, tracking objects, delay, connectivity)
- Troubleshoot NetFlow (v5, v9, flexible NetFlow)
- Troubleshoot network problems using Cisco DNA Center assurance (connectivity, monitoring, device health, network health)

Troubleshoot device management

Console and VTY

CTY is your console port. On any router, it appears in the router configuration as line con <#>.

VTY lines are virtual terminal lines of a router and are used primarily to control inbound telnet or SSH connections. You can configure them by using line vty 0 <#> command.

Telnet, HTTP, HTTPS, SSH, SCP, (T)FTP

Telecommunication Network (or Telnet) is a well-known communication protocol that is used to connect into a networking device with a virtual terminal interface. It offers character-based access to another system. All telnet sessions are generally authenticated using a locally configured credentials (user id and password) or ones that are validated via AAA server.

Telnet uses TCP for transport and operates over port #23.

Secure Shell (or SSH) provides a secure way to access one computer (the server) from another (the client). SSH protocol uses session keys that are derived using DH key exchange or ECDH. Once both systems agree on a key, it can be used to encrypt the session using an encryption algorithm such as AES.

SSH uses TCP for protocol transport and operates over port #22.

Hyper Text Transfer Protocol (HTTP) is the protocol for the web communication. It defines how web messages are formatted and what actions both browsers and web servers perform in response to various verbs.

HTTP uses TCP for transport and operates over port #80.

HTTPS is an encrypted version of HTTP using the SSL certificate. HTTPs can also make use of Transport Layer Security (or TLS). HTTPS, like HTTP, uses TCP for transport and operates over port #443.

FTP is another client/server protocol that can be used to transfer files between two computer systems. Trivial FTP (or TFTP) is yet another file transfer protocol. FTP is secure whereas TFTP is not. FTP uses TCP for protocol transport whereas TFTP uses UDP. FTP uses TCP port 20 and 21 whereas TFTP uses UDP port 69.

SFTP and FTPS are also example of secure file transfer protocols, where SFTP uses SSH and FTPS uses SSL/TLS for authentication and encryption.

Secure Copy (or SCP) is another file transfer protocols that can be used between a local (the client) and a remote host (the server). SCP uses SSH to provide authentication and encryption. SCP, like SSH, uses TCP for protocol transport and operates over port #22.

Troubleshoot SNMP (v2c, v3)

SNMP has been around for over 30 years. Over this time, it has been the de-facto way to monitor networks. It worked great when networks were small and polling a device every 15-30 minutes met operational requirements. SNMP MIBs are a type of data model defining a collection of information that is organized in a hierarchical format that is used along with SNMP. Anyhow, SNMP did work great for monitoring devices every few minutes, but it never caught on for configuration management purposes due to custom or proprietary MIBs.

In addition to SNMP, there has always been the network command line interface or CLI. Access to the CLI happens via console, Telnet, or SSH, and it has been the de-facto way of managing configuration of networking devices for the past 20+ years. If you tally up the way devices have been managed for 20 years, you can see that there has been no good way to handle machine to machine mechanism i.e. using software to configure network devices.

SNMPv2c is identical to SNMPv1 except it expands the counters to 64-bit (4.29B) long. This helps a lot with avoiding overlap when working with high speed interfaces. SNMPv3 adds a layer of security to SNMPv2c by adding both authentication and encryption which can be used together or one at a time.

SNMPv3 authentication provides security for SNMP traps, so as messages are created they are assigned a special key that is based on the EngineID of the entity. This key is also shared with the receiver or the management workstation to verify the message integrity. SNMPv3 also provides encryption so SNMP traps can't be modified while in transit to the receiver.

Troubleshoot network problems using logging (local, syslog, debugs, conditional debugs, timestamps)

Cisco IOS CLI is packed with tools (much like Linux) that allow you to view and troubleshoot the current state of the overall system. This is true regardless of the actual IOS variant, i.e. whether that's now-defunct classic IOS, or IOS XE or IOS XR. Primarily, there are two tools within Cisco IOS that stand out more than all others and they are show and debug commands.

While show commands provide you with a one-time snapshot of the current system state for a specific area such "show ip route" for routing, debug commands on the other hand, provide you with real-time details of the system innerworkings (e.g. debug ip packet) until they are explicitly turned off by the network admin. For this reason alone, you need to run debugs with caution. Debug commands that operate on every packet, as opposed to specific events, can be intense for the router's CPU.

You can minimize the debug CPU overhead by narrowing down the scope of the debug command, a feature that's known as conditional debugging. Conditional debugging allows you to filter out the debug information shown by the interface and/or the conditions that you specify.

You can start a debug command simply by just entering and executing the command for your specific area of interest such as IP routing, OSPF or BGP or NetFlow etc. Now, regardless of the number of debug commands you've running at any moment, Cisco has made it easier to shut them all down by using one single command, i.e. "no debug all" or "undebug all". You can also display set of all debugs that are configured on a given system using the "show debug" command. Under default configuration, debug output is sent only to console port. Cisco recommends that you disable this default by using "no logging console" command. You can turn on debug output on an SSH or Telnet session by using the "terminal monitor" command. If you don't witness any command output despite entering "terminal monitor" command, be sure to verify that "no logging on" command has not been used. You can also log debug messages to a memory buffer using "logging buffered" command.

Before you use debug command(s), Cisco recommends that you configure millisecond level timestamping on the router, for debug and logs, by using the following commands.

router(config)#service timestamps debug datetime msec
router(config)#service timestamps log datetime msec

When using debug on a platform that runs Cisco IOS XE, keep in mind the following additional guidelines.

- Show debug condition (shows all conditional debugs)
- Show platform condition (shows platform conditional debugs and state)
- Debug platform condition start | stop (starts or stops the platform conditional debugging)
- Clear platform condition all (removes the debug conditions applied to the platform)

Cisco IOS XE Conditional Debugging Examples

The following example shows how to enable debugging for packets matching an ACL 101 and destination IPv4 address 100.1.1.1 on interface Gi0/1/2, and to enable conditional debug for the CEF-MPLS feature:

Router# access-list 100 permit ip any 100.1.1.1
Router# debug platform condition interface Gi0/1/2 access-list 101
Router# debug platform condition feature cef-mpls datapath level info
Router# debug platform condition start

The following example shows how to enable debug for packets matching an ACL 200, matching mpls packets with a label of 20, on interface Gi0/1/2, and to enable conditional debug for the CEF-MPLS feature:

Router# access-list 20 permit any 20 any any
Router# debug platform condition interface Gi0/1/2 access-list 200
Router# debug platform condition feature cef-mpls datapath
Router# debug platform condition start

Remote logging via syslog is a crucial tool for root cause analysis that necessitates debug captures from a router and more over long periods of time. There is virtually no limit to how many debug log entries you can generate and send to remote syslog servers.

Configuring Syslog

It is Cisco's recommended best practice to configure timestamping on all the routers involved in debugging, since it makes it easier to corroborate log entries across routers.

Logging <syslog-server-IP-address> allows you to configure syslog-based logging on a Cisco router. You can also specify multiple syslog destinations.

Logging trap <level #> command specifies the type of messages by severity level that you want to be sent to the syslog server. The default severity is informational (#6) and lower which includes Debug output (#7). However, you can configure it to be all the way down to 0 which essentially means sent everything to syslog so obviously proceed with caution.

Logging facility <facility-type> lets you specify the facility level used by the syslog. The default is local7 whereas possible values go from local0 to local7.

```
Router#config terminal
Enter configuration commands, one per line. End with CNTL/Z.
Router(config)#logging 192.168.1.10
Router(config)#service timestamps debug datetime localtime show-timezone msec
Router(config)#service timestamps log datetime localtime show-timezone msec
Router(config)#logging facility local4
Router(config)#logging trap warning
Router(config)#end
```

Verifying Syslog

You can verify syslog by using the "show logging" command.

```
Router#show logging
Syslog logging: enabled (0 messages dropped, 0 flushes, 0 overruns)
    Console logging: level debugging, 79 messages logged
    Monitor logging: level debugging, 0 messages logged
    Buffer logging: disabled
    Trap logging: level warnings, 80 message lines logged
       Logging to 192.168.1.10, 57 message lines logged
```

Troubleshoot IPv4 and IPv6 DHCP (DHCP client, IOS DHCP server, DHCP relay, DHCP options)

Dynamic Host Configuration Protocol (or DHCP) is used for assigning IP addresses to any IP devices that are configured as DHCP clients. By default, the

IP address assignment is dynamic however the DHCP server can be configured to hand out a pre-assigned or static IP address based on the device's MAC address.

All Cisco IOS XE devices can server as DHCP servers. During the address assignment, a DHCP server can also be configured to provide DHCP option values. These options can include information such as subnet mask, gateway, NTP server, Hostname, TFTP server name, DHCP relay agent information etc.

In case of DHCPv6, likewise there are a number of options available.

- Vendor specific information option
- TFTP server addresses
- Syslog server addresses
- DNS recursive name server
- FQDN option

Troubleshoot network performance issues using IP SLA (jitter, tracking objects, delay, connectivity)

Cisco IP SLA sends data across the network to simulate actual network data and collects network performance information in real time. IP SLA measurements can be used for troubleshooting and for network planning and design.

IP SLA can be configured to report on the following crucial network parameters.

- Jitter
- Response time
- Packet loss
- Mean Opinion Score (or MOS) for voice quality
- Connectivity
- Delay

IP SLA is a layer 3 feature thus can be configured end to end to best reflect the metrics close to what an end user might experience.

IP SLA Configuration

In order to configure IP SLA, you need to perform the following tasks.

1. Enable IP SLA Responder(s)
2. Configure IP SLA operation type
3. Configure any options as needed for your operation type
4. Configure threshold conditions
5. Schedule the operation to run
6. Display and read results either using show CLIs or via SNMP

ICMP Echo Operation Example

The following ICMP echo operation will start immediately and run indefinitely.

```
ip sla 6
 icmp-echo 172.29.139.134 source-ip 172.29.139.132
 frequency 300
 request-data-size 28
 tos 160
 timeout 2000
 tag SFO-RO
ip sla schedule 6 life forever start-time now
```

UDP Echo Operation Example

The UDP echo operation measures end to end response time between a Cisco device and any other device simple configured with an IP address. The following UDP echo operation will start immediately and run indefinitely.

```
ip sla 5
 udp-echo 172.29.139.134 5000
 frequency 30
 request-data-size 160
 tos 128
 timeout 1000
 tag FLL-RO
ip sla schedule 5 life forever start-time now
```

IP SLA Verification

show ip sla group schedule, displays IP SLA group schedule details

show ip sla configuration, displays IP SLA configuration

Troubleshoot NetFlow (v5, v9, flexible NetFlow)

NetFlow is a Cisco IOS feature that provides detailed statistics for packets flowing through a router. NetFlow data capture helps capture data in the form of incoming or outgoing packets. A flow is identified as a directional stream of packets between a source and a destination based on a combination of network (such as source/destination IP addresses), transport layer information (such as source/destination TCP or UDP ports), L3 protocol type, Type of Service (ToS) and input interface.

Typical use cases for NetFlow include network or application monitoring, application profiling, network planning, aid in DDoS mitigation, and data warehousing.

Ingress IP packets include IP to IP and IP to MPLS packets, whereas Egress IP packets likewise include IP to IP and MPLS to IP packets.

NetFlow Interface Support for Ingress (Received) Traffic on an interface

```
configure terminal
!
interface ethernet 0/0
 ip flow ingress
!
```

NetFlow Interface Support for Egress (Transmitted) Traffic on an Interface

```
configure terminal
```

```
!
interface ethernet 1/0
 ip flow egress
```

NetFlow Flow Export Destination and Version

NetFlow data export destination is a host that's running an application that can collect NetFlow data. NetFlow data export version 9 is a flexible format and supports new fields and record types needed to accommodate BGP next hop and MPLS protocol support.

```
Router(config)# ip flow-export destination 192.168.1.10
Router(config)# ip flow-export version 9
```

Verifying NetFlow Configuration

To verify, if NetFlow is working properly, you can use any of the following show commands.

```
Show ip cache flow
Show ip cache verbose flow
Show ip flow interface
```

```
Router# show ip cache flow
IP packet size distribution (1103746 total packets):
   1-32   64   96  128  160  192  224  256  288  320  352  384  416  448  480
   .249 .694 .000 .000 .000 .000 .000 .000 .000 .000 .000 .000 .000 .000 .000
   512  544  576 1024 1536 2048 2560 3072 3584 4096 4608
   .000 .000 .027 .000 .027 .000 .000 .000 .000 .000 .000
IP Flow Switching Cache, 278544 bytes
  35 active, 4061 inactive, 980 added
  2921778 ager polls, 0 flow alloc failures
  Active flows timeout in 30 minutes
  Inactive flows timeout in 15 seconds
```

```
IP Sub Flow Cache, 21640 bytes
  0 active, 1024 inactive, 0 added, 0 added to flow
  0 alloc failures, 0 force free
  1 chunk, 1 chunk added
  last clearing of statistics never
Protocol        Total   Flows  Packets Bytes  Packets Active(Sec) Idle(Sec)
--------        Flows   /Sec   /Flow /Pkt    /Sec   /Flow    /Flow
TCP-FTP          208    0.0    1133   40     2.4   1799.6      0.9
TCP-FTPD         208    0.0    1133   40     2.4   1799.6      0.9
TCP-WWW           14    0.0    1133   40     1.2   1799.6      0.8
TCP-SMTP          14    0.0    1133   40     1.2   1799.6      0.8
TCP-BGP           17    0.0    1133   40     0.6   1799.6      0.7
TCP-NNTP          17    0.0    1133   40     0.6   1799.6      0.7
TCP-other         97    0.0    1133   40     6.8   1799.7      0.8
UDP-TFTP          17    0.0    1133   28     0.6   1799.6      1.0
UDP-other        508    0.0    1417   28     3.1   1799.6      0.9
ICMP             235    0.0    1133  427     3.1   1799.6      0.8
Total:          1335    0.0    1166   91    22.4   1799.6      0.8
SrcIf      SrcIPaddress  DstIf      DstIPaddress  Pr SrcP DstP  Pkts
<output truncated for brevity>
```

To verify, if the NetFlow data export is operational or not, you can use "show ip flow export" command.

```
Router# show ip flow export
Flow export v9 is enabled for main cache
  Exporting flows to 192.168.10.2 (1000)
  Exporting using source interface Ethernet0/1
  Version 9 flow records
  0 flows exported in 0 udp datagrams
  0 flows failed due to lack of export packet
  0 export packets were sent up to process level
  0 export packets were dropped due to no fib
  0 export packets were dropped due to adjacency issues
```

0 export packets were dropped due to fragmentation failures
0 export packets were dropped due to encapsulation fixup failures

The newer form of NetFlow is known as Flexible NetFlow (or FNF), it allows you to understand network behavior for more specific applications by allowing you to define new flow keys for packet length or MAC address.

Flexible NetFlow consists of several components including flow records, flow monitors, flow exporters and flow samplers. Flow records are a combination of key and non-key fields. Flow records are assigned to flow monitors to define the flow data cache. You can either use pre-defined flow records or create your own. Flow monitors are applied to interfaces and carry data collected within the cache. Flow exporters export the flow monitor cache to external NetFlow collection hosts. Flow samplers are used to reduce the load on the device by sampling packets (1 out of n). Samplers are combined with flow monitors as they are applied to an interface.

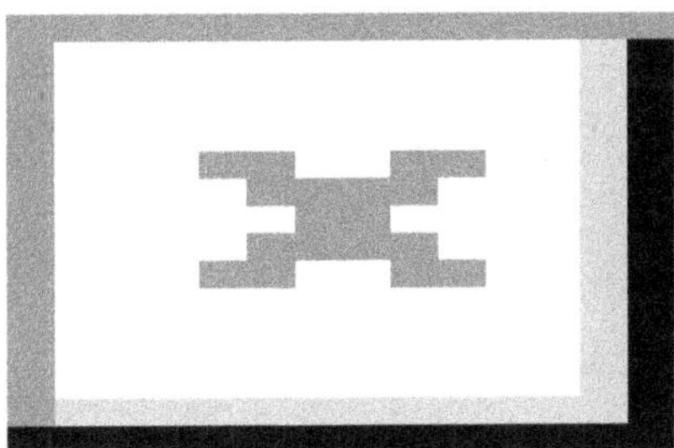

Creating a Flow Record

Router(config)# flow record FR1

Router(config-flow-record)# match ipv4 destination address

Router# show flow record
flow record FR1:
  Description: Used for basic IPv4 traffic analysis
  No. of users: 1
  Total field space: 129 bytes
  Fields:
    match ipv4 destination address
    collect counter bytes
    collect counter packets

Creating a Flow Monitor

Router(config)# flow monitor FR1
Router(config-flow-monitor)# record netflow ipv4 original-input

Creating a Flow Exporter

Router(config)# flow exporter FEX1
Router(config-flow-exporter)# destination 192.168.1.2
Router(config-flow-exporter)# export-protocol netflow-v9
Router(config-flow-exporter)# transport udp 65

Router(config)# flow monitor FR1
Router(config-flow-monitor)# exporter FEX1

Verifying Data in the Flow Monitor Cache

Router# show flow monitor name FR1 cache format record

Cache type: Normal

  Current entries: 4

```
High Watermark:                          4
Flows added:                      101
Flows aged:                       97
  - Active timeout  ( 1800 secs)       3
  - Inactive timeout (   15 secs)       94
  - Event aged                 0
  - Watermark aged                0
  - Emergency aged                0
IPV4 DESTINATION ADDRESS:  192.168.1.2
ipv4 source address:      100.10.11.1
trns source port:      25
trns destination port:   25
counter bytes:        72840
counter packets:       1821
```

Troubleshoot network problems using Cisco DNA Center assurance (connectivity, monitoring, device health, network health)

Cisco DNA Center is at the center of Cisco's intent-based networking initiative. Cisco customers and partners can use APIs, integration flows, events and notification services and Cisco DNA Center SDK to create applications above and beyond the features it natively provides.

Cisco DNA center is controller as well as an analytics platform that makes Cisco's intent-based networking possible. It consists of five major components.

- Design
- Policy
- Provision
- Assurance
- Platform

DNA Center Dashboard

DNA Design component allows you to design your network using workflows while allowing for importing existing network designs and device images from APIC-EM (Enterprise Module) and Cisco Prime Infrastructure into DNA Center.

DNA Policy is about user and device profiles that help deliver on secure access as well as segmentation. Application policies ensure consistent network performance based on business requirements.

DNA Provision allows you to use policy-based automation to deliver services to network-based on business priority and simplifies device deployment. It is the module that is responsible for delivering zero-touch deployment.

DNA Assurance enables networking elements to stream telemetry for ensuring application performance and user connectivity in real-time.

DNA Platform allows developers to directly access the DNA through the developer toolkit or SDK. In order to review APIs, you can click on Platform > Developer Toolkit.

DNA center appliance hosts SDN controller, analytics engine and telemetry storage. At the time of writing, 44-core DNA appliance (DN2-HW-APL) is listed for $88.6K USD in Cisco's GPL. It must be installed and run on bundled bare metal server, currently there is no virtual appliance package available.

DNA center licenses come in three flavors, i.e.

- Essentials (includes basic automation and network visibility)
- Advantage (includes Essentials, plus advanced automation, image lifecycle management, AI/ML analytics and assurance and API/SDK integration)

- Premier (Everything in Advantage, plus encrypted traffic analytics and multi-domain policy segmentation)

Let's now look at various aspects of DNA dashboard and types of data it provides.

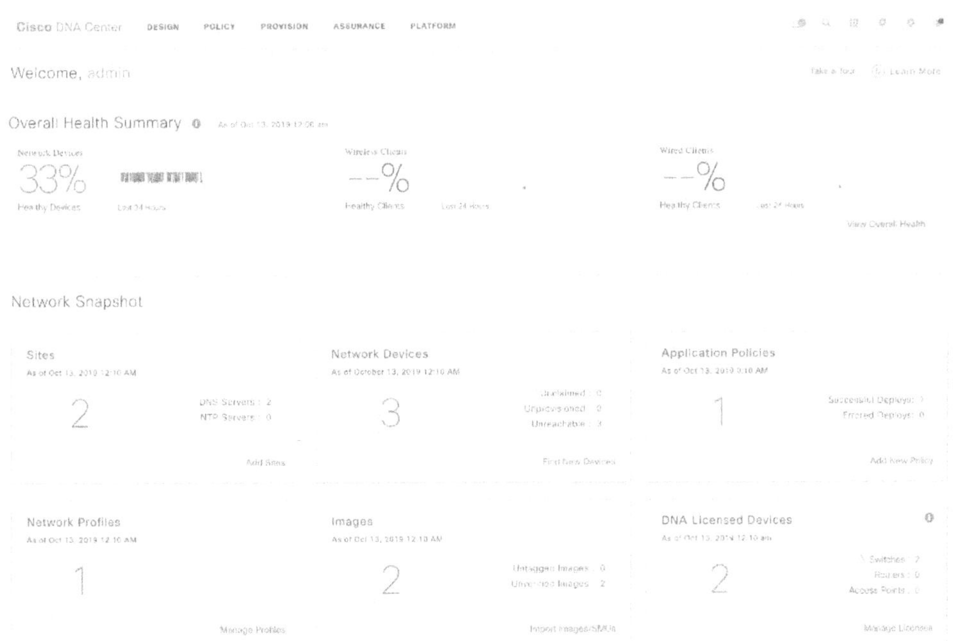

Let's now get our hands dirty with DNA center SDK by using the python client module.

Cisco DNA Center   DESIGN   POLICY   PROVISION   ASSURANCE   PLATFORM

Platform   Version 1.0.3 - Released 2/8/2019

Overview   Manage ∨   **Developer Toolkit** ∨   Runtime Dashboard

APIs

> Know Your Network

> Site Management

> Connectivity

> Operational Tools

Authentication

APIs
Integration Flows
Data and Reports
Multivendor support

Know your Network APIs can be used to discover details about clients, sites, topology and devices. It also provides programmatic REST APIs to add devices to the network and export device data.

Sites

Method	Name	Description	
GET	Get Site Health	Returns Overall Health information for all sites	...
POST	Assign Device To Site	Assigns list of devices to a site	...
POST	Create Site Point	Creates site with area/building/floor with specified hierarchy.	...

Networks

Method	Name	Description	
GET	Get VLAN details	Returns the list of VLAN names	...
GET	Get Site Topology	Returns site topology	...
GET	Get L3 Topology Details	Returns the Layer 3 network topology by routing protocol	...

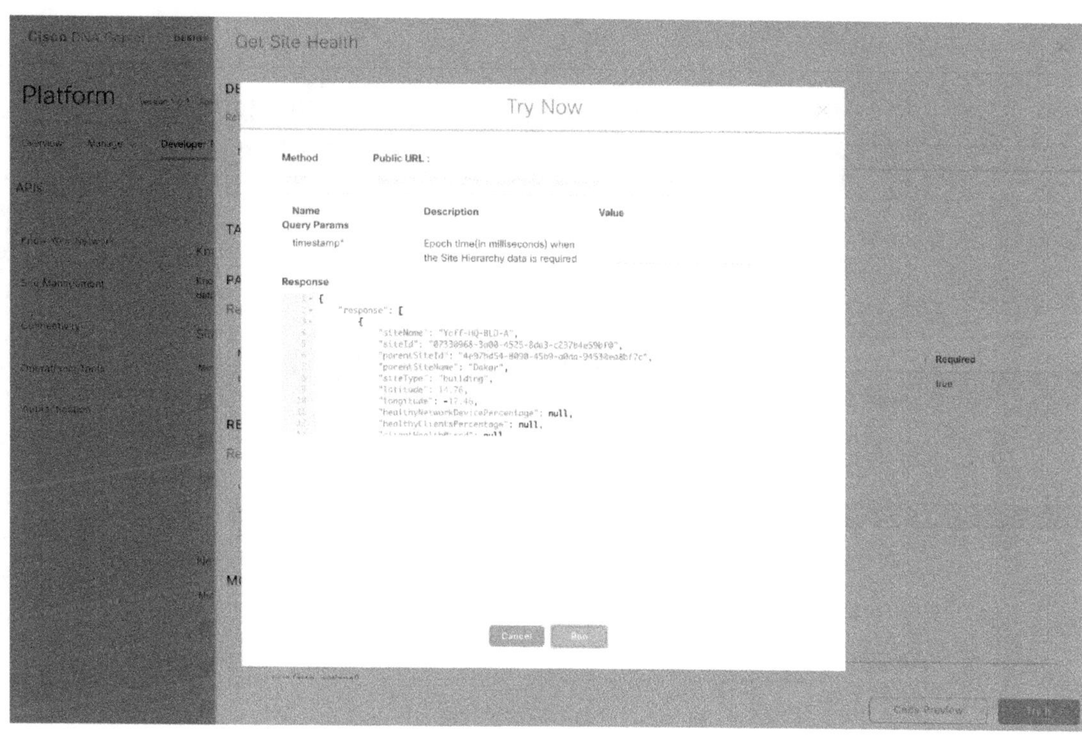
Cisco DNA Center
Get Site Health
Platform
Try Now
Method   Public URL :
Name   Description   Value
Query Params
timestamp*   Epoch time(in milliseconds) when
              the Site Hierarchy data is required
Response
Cancel   Run

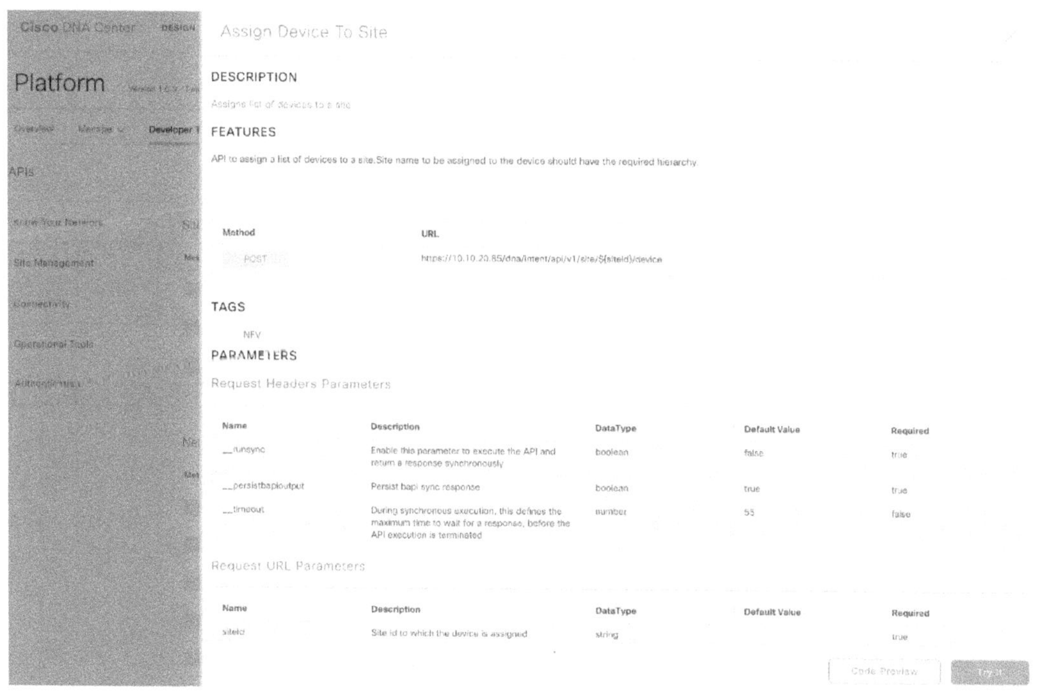
Cisco DNA Center   DESIGN
Assign Device To Site
Platform
DESCRIPTION
Assigns list of devices to a site.
FEATURES
API to assign a list of devices to a site. Site name to be assigned to the device should have the required hierarchy.
Method   URL
POST   https://10.10.20.85/dna/intent/api/v1/site/${siteId}/device
TAGS
NFV
PARAMETERS
Request Headers Parameters
Name   Description   DataType   Default Value   Required
__runsync   Enable this parameter to execute the API and   boolean   false   true
                return a response synchronously
__persistbapioutput   Persist bapi sync response   boolean   true   true
__timeout   During synchronous execution, this defines the   number   55   false
                maximum time to wait for a response, before the
                API execution is terminated
Request URL Parameters
Name   Description   DataType   Default Value   Required
siteId   Site id to which the device is assigned   string   true
Code Preview   Try It

Creating a site.

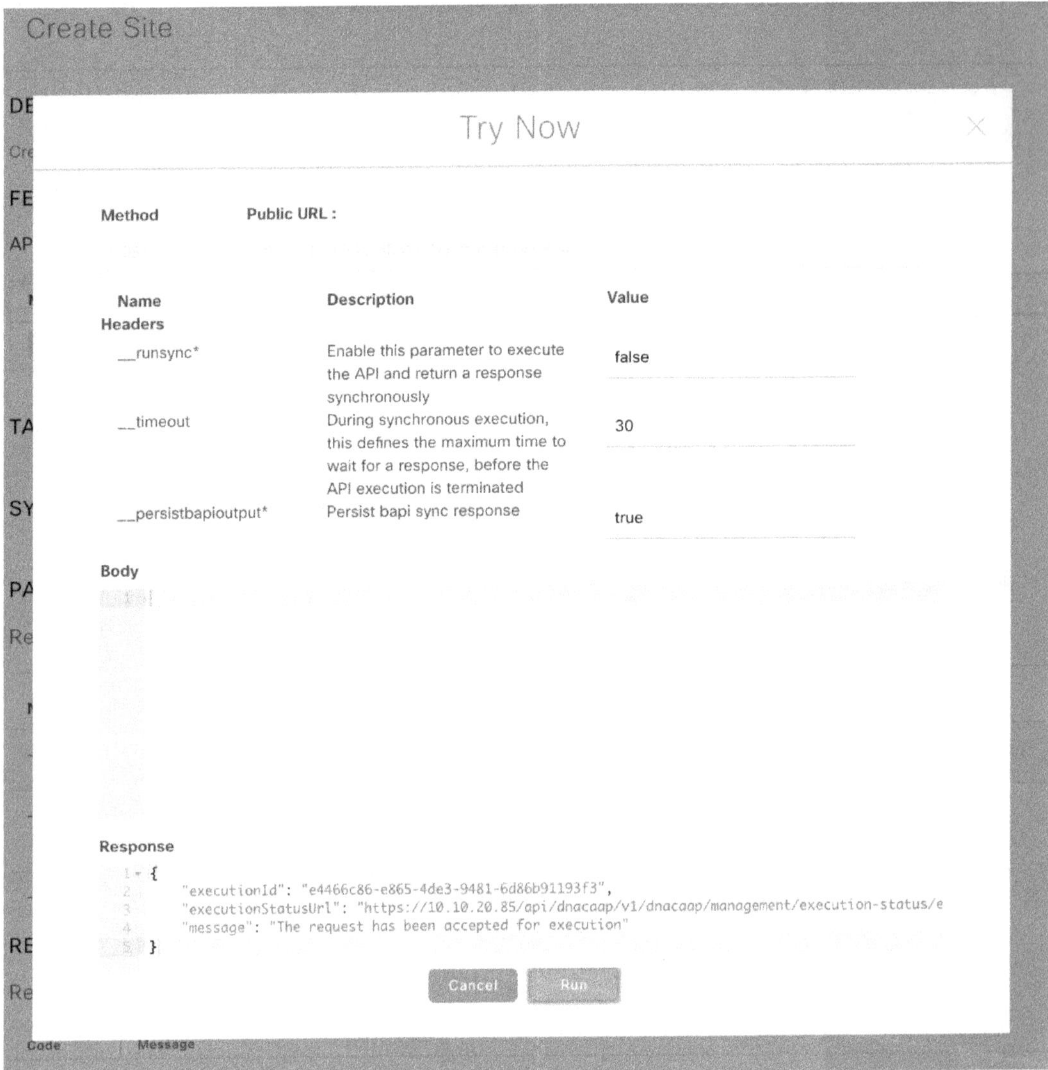

Toolkit provides information about all of the API calls that are part of the SDK. However, before we proceed further, let me summarize the types of APIs that are available with the DNA Center.

- Northbound APIs
- Southbound APIs

- Eastbound APIs
- Westbound APIs

Northbound APIs, also known as, Intent APIs provide support for policy-based abstraction of business intent, allowing focus on business outcomes as opposed to mechanics of how. It is a RESTful APIs that allows use of GET, POST, PUT and DELETE HTTP methods with JSON encoding to discover and control the network. All API calls require use of a security token that identifies the privileges of an authenticated user making the RESTful API calls. You must obtain a security token before you can make use of any of the DNA center APIs.

Southbound APIs allows managing non-Cisco infrastructure by way of SDK that allow creation of packages for 3rd party devices. Package contains mapping of Cisco DNA center features to other vendors' southbound protocols. In summary, southbound APIs are a gateway to multivendor support within Cisco DNA center.

Events and Notifications provide the ability to establish a notification handler, so when specific DNA center events are triggered, such as SoftWare Image Management (SWIM) events, 3rd party systems can take actions in response to those events. Notifications can also be generated for internal events such as Assurance event causing an external ITSM system to initiate a ticket.

Westbound APIs, or what's also known as Integration APIs, are provided so that other 3rd party systems such as ITSM can be integrated with Cisco DNA center. Using integration APIs, you can implement change management, and approval and pre-approval chains. They also allow integration for reporting and analytics capabilities such as capacity planning, asset management, compliance control and auditing. Finally, integration APIs allow support for IT4IT reference architecture so if you are using an external system that supports that, you can be sure to optimize your end-to-end IT value chain.

You can use DNA Center to monitor and troubleshoot network health. In DNA center, a network consists of one or more devices which includes routers, switches, APs, and WLCs. DNA Center doesn't use clients or end users as part of the network health score as expected.

In order to look at Network Health, you need to browse to Assurance > Health > Network.

The health of the network devices is represented with four colors.

1. Gray means No Data available. Score is 0.
2. Red means critical issues. Score ranges from 1 to 3.
3. Orange means Warnings. Score ranges from 4 to 7.
4. Green means No Errors or warning. Score ranges from 8 to 10.

Network health score represents the proportion of the number of the healthy devices. If your network has 10 devices in total and 5 of them have a health score of 8-10 (Green) then your network health is at 50%.

In order to look at Health of a Device, you need to browse to Assurance > Health > Network Health then click a Device name in the device column or search a device using its name or IP/MAC address.

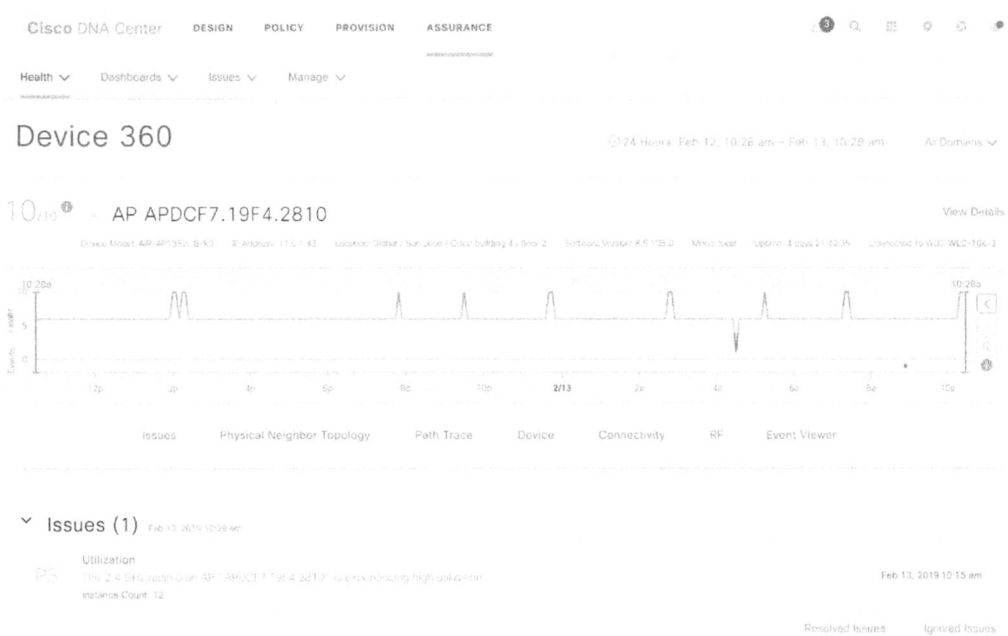

Individual device health score is the minimum score of the various KPIs that are available for the device.

Device Health Score = Minimum of (system health, data plane connectivity, control plane connectivity)

System, data and control planes health score take various metrics into account depending on whether a device is a switch, or wireless controller or an AP, or a router, or a Fabric. For example, for a switch, system monitoring metrics such as CPU utilization and memory usage count towards health score.